"A VERY SPECIAL BOOK—
INSTRUCTIVE,
INFORMATIVE,
REASSURING,
IMPRESSIVE—
JUST LIKE ITS AUTHOR!"

—Dick Schaap

Dr. Theodore Isaac Rubin is known to readers throughout the country for his column in the *Ladies' Home
Journal* and his bestselling books, among them *Lisa
and David* (on which the film *David and Lisa* was
based) and *Compassion and Self Hate*. He is President
of the American Institute for Psychoanalysis, where he
is also a training and supervising analyst, and is on the
boards of the Karen Horney Clinic and other distin-
guished psychiatric organizations. Dr. Rubin is married,
with three children, and lives in New York City.

THEODORE ISAAC RUBIN, M.D.

Reconciliations

INNER PEACE IN AN AGE OF ANXIETY

BERKLEY BOOKS, NEW YORK

This Berkley book contains the complete
text of the original hardcover edition.
It has been completely reset in a typeface
designed for easy reading, and was printed
from new film.

RECONCILIATIONS:
Inner Peace in an Age of Anxiety

A Berkley Book / published by arrangement with
The Viking Press

PRINTING HISTORY
Viking edition / August 1980
Berkley edition / September 1982
Third printing / September 1983

ISBN: 0-425-06312-7

A BERKLEY BOOK ® TM 757,375
Berkley Books are published by The Berkley Publishing Group,
200 Madison Avenue, New York, New York 10016.
The name "BERKLEY" and the stylized "B" with design
are trademarks belonging to Berkley Publishing Corporation.
PRINTED IN THE UNITED STATES OF AMERICA

In memory of two Nathans—my father,
Nathan Rubin, and my analyst, Nat Freeman—
        and
in celebration of my granddaughter,
        Nathania.

CONTENTS

PREFACE

IN THIS BOOK I am concerned with reconciliations with one's self, all aspects of the human condition, and the inescapable world we live in.

Reconciling is a mending and integrating process. It involves bringing aspects of self, and of self and others, together into relative mutual harmony. This is the antithesis of one aspect giving way to the other or of one being sacrificed for the other. For reconciliation to take place, blind compulsivity, pride, inner tyranny, and self-glorification must be reduced as insight, humility, and humanity are increased.

The term "mellow" is used occasionally, because in our current vernacular this term best describes the mood and feel of reconciliation. I believe that through reconciliation of the kind described here one's self is strengthened so that inner peace becomes a possibility.

The book is divided into three sections. It is helpful to our purpose but not mandatory to read them in sequence.

Theodore Isaac Rubin, M.D.
New York, September 1979

A HUMAN BEING is a part of the whole, called by us "Universe," a part limited in time and space. He experiences himself, his thoughts and feelings as something separated from the rest—a kind of optical illusion of his consciousness. This delusion is a kind of prison for us, restricting us to our personal desires and to affection for a few persons nearest to us. Our task must be to free ourselves from this prison by widening our circle of compassion to embrace all living creatures and the whole of nature in its beauty. Nobody is able to achieve this completely, but the striving for such achievement is in itself a part of the liberation and a foundation for inner security.

—*Albert Einstein*

PART I

THE BASIC PHILOSOPHY

1.

CULTURE KILLS

OUR CULTURE, WITH its values and pressures, kills time, energy, spontaneity, pleasure, sensibilities, creativity, vitality, aliveness, feelings, humanity, and life itself. Our society is a glory-seeking, pride-oriented dynamic system, which influences each family to influence each newborn child to predicate his or her self-acceptance on where he or she lands in the self-glorification hierarchy. Simply put, this means that we accept ourselves almost exclusively in terms of achievement and "success," as it is measured by money, prestige, power, sexual attractiveness, or youth.

Most of us consciously and unconsciously suffer because we feel we *ought* to have or *must* attain all the qualities and achievements society tells us we should. And since the ideal of success is impossible to attain—let alone to sustain—and success is never enough, however much of it *is* attained, self-hate and misery inevitably ensue.

To compensate for lack of "success" and the lack of self-acceptance that goes with it, many of us resort to neurotic stratagems: we deaden our feelings; we withdraw from life's realistic offerings and benefits; we seek glory through martyrdom; we try to achieve vindictive

3

triumphs over our fellows; we are compulsively compliant, obsessively conformist, and malignantly self-effacing in an effort to be universally loved—the list goes on and on. A life lived on these terms is largely one of chronic misery interposed with synthetic "highs" based on momentary "victories." It is a life of inner emptiness, a cemetery of dead feelings haunted by a chronic, confused yearning for an impossible, unknown, never-arriving magic *something* that would give meaning to existence.

On a national and international level, it could be said that catering to pride and glory adds up to war, famine, waste, depletion of natural resources, and, ultimately, to species extinction. Certainly on an individual physiological level, this pressure syndrome can lead to cerebral strokes, crippling heart attacks, and early deaths, and men and women who "resign" in defeat can become self-hating enough to suffer an onslaught of self-destructive, painful, crippling, and often death-dealing psychosomatic repercussions.

As the great psychoanalyst Karen Horney recognized, there is an enormous difference betweeen compulsive self-glorification and the free choice involved in healthy self-realization. She documented and brilliantly elucidated the dynamics and destructive aspects of sick pride. But knowing the dangers of stressful competitiveness is not enough. What can we do to save our lives and to enjoy our time on this remarkable planet? The answer lies partly in an understanding of what and where we are as a species.

Beyond Instincts

If our behavior, like that of many other creatures on earth, is simply a pattern of responses to inborn chemical demands and signposts, however well disguised, then we are helpless, and even doomed—as have been other instinct-driven creatures now largely vanished from the surface of this planet.

If Freud was right, and if culture and, indeed, all human activity are based on nothing more than sublimated instinctual drives, then it would be purposeless to entertain the possibility of a different philosophical design for living. The same is true if the Darwinian law of biological competition and survival of the fittest still applies to our species. But I believe otherwise.

Of course we started out as simple instinctual creatures. We too were servants of our own biology. Chemical signposts inherent in our genes directed our behavior. And a great part of this behavior was involved with competition with other members of our species as part of a selective breeding process through which only the fittest would survive. Our current competitive culture is a relic of these biological drives characteristic of our forefathers thousands of generations ago.

But *now* we are no longer the creatures we were *then*. I believe that human beings (alone of all species) have transcended the dictates of biochemical instinct—their very biochemistry has evolved to a point where that chemistry frees them from their chemistry. We have an enormous range of adaptation possibilities, but, unfortunately, we don't know this on a fully conscious level. We continue to live with values of much simpler creatures, rationalizing them with arguments of "territorial imperatives," racial superiority, or economic need.

We so often hear that our principal difficulty as a society is that a huge and dangerous gap exists between our technological and social advances, and the potential for destruction in a species whose members relate primitively, but invent machines for destruction light-years ahead of their social development, is obvious. But the real rootgap, if we may call it that, is rather between a very advanced biology and a primitive sociology.

Our sociological progress simply has not kept up with

our biological pace. Unless we allow ourselves to catch up—more than that, unless we struggle valiantly to catch up—we must face catastrophe. We are no longer dealing with simple forces and Stone Age men. On a global level, our competitive strivings involve men who control destructive power of immense magnitude; and on an individual basis also, our capacity for self-destruction in the race for self-glorification is almost unlimited. Fortunately, our potential for survival is just as strong.

For me the development of medical science, with its implications for relieving pain and prolonging life, provides much evidence of how far we've come: fitness and survival are now functions of choice, not the inevitable result of naked competition.

A man whose sense of reality was 10,000 years old—who carried a club as he looked for his lunch in the middle of Times Square at noon—would be considered psychotic, because he retained a delusion that saber-toothed tigers exist and provide the most convenient meal. Considering the extent to which we have evolved as a species, would we be remiss to call our culture psychotic? If we do, doesn't it deserve the most serious application of remedial treatment? But we must deal with the individual brain—or mind, if you will. Then what about this brain? And can the gap between our advanced biology and primitive sociology be closed? Is there choice and can this choice be exercised? How important really is it for man to stop competing for glory, to give up the inappropriate fight for survival of the fittest—this residual of a time long since past?

"Take It Easy"

I don't know exactly when or how it began and for a long time I certainly did not know why. But some years ago, instead of saying "Good-bye" to people, I almost invariably said, "Take it easy." Maybe I picked it up from a book, a movie, or a radio actor; in any case the expression became my "good-bye" and for years I ascribed no special meaning to it.

But gradually, stimulated by psychoanalytic treatment, I realized that while I was trying to tell others something, the major message was really to myself. There was something I was trying to break through and to convey to myself. Years later when I wrote *Compassion and Self Hate* I knew there was a connection between the expression "Take it easy" and the book, especially the last third of the book, called "On Human Terms."

Like nearly everyone else, I too have been inundated by the cultural value system we live in. There are very few of the multifaceted illusions and pressures connected to the success/pride syndrome that I've escaped. Indeed, as I described at the beginning of *Compassion and Self Hate*, I initially went into analytic treatment because of a severe depressive reaction. This was due to severely hurt pride and resulting intense self-hate. It is interesting that most of us consider depression following "personal failure" (a business reversal due to a bad decision, poor results on a state board or bar or other licensing exam, inability to land a job, whatever) as appropriate. (Even the psychiatric profession regards some depressions as "appropriate" and others as "inappropriate.")

This tendency reveals how brainwashed we are into believing that success deserves self-acceptance and that failure deserves self-rejection, self-hate, and depression. The fact is that depression following personal failure is *inappropriate* in terms of the basic realities of life. In terms of life's realities, the only reactions appropriate to personal failure are: 1) unsurprised recognition that failure is a common occurrence in the human experience, and 2) sympathy for self and the human condition generally. That we consider depression—even self-re-

crimination—appropriate following personal failure is
an indication of the strength of the emotional strangle-
hold our malignant culture has on us.

This belief in the "appropriateness" of self-hate and
depression touches our conception of the human condition in general. It is a belief that denies human limitations and hates people for being human; that sees sickness as failure, death as failure, aging as failure, lack of
ambition to destroy one's fellows in "sport," business,
or war as failure, lack of interest in material acquisition
as failure, lack of pleasure in conquest as failure. This is
an outlook that finds a million justifiable reasons for
killing one's own spirit and real self and those of one's
children and one's fellows through countless personal
assaults—not to mention that psychotic public assault
we call war.

It was this destructive value system that I was trying
to exorcise with the term "Take it easy." I sensed that
our culture's values had removed me from me—from
spontaneity, aliveness, and real feelings. How peculiar
to stand up and to struggle against inner tyranny with
the slogan "Take it easy" rather than with "Keep
punching," "Stay in there," or "Hit them where it
hurts"! But it was no more peculiar than Gandhi's
"fighting" the military might of Great Britain with
passive resistance. I was trying to tell myself and others
to offer passive resistance to the demands of society.
Perhaps this is the message people are unconsciously
trying to deliver to themselves and others when they say
"Cool it" or "Relax." If I had drawn up a plan of
resistance, it might have included these steps:

1) *Stop the pursuit of the mythical "it"*—that
nonexistent, self-glorifying, heaven-producing magical
"something" we sometimes mistakenly call our "real
self," which couldn't have less to do with either reality
or self.

2) *Stop running in the rat race for success.* Stand still long enough to become conscious of self and feelings other than lows and highs connected to failures and victories.

3) *Get a feeling of yourself in the immediate world again*—looking at and really seeing other people's faces, buildings, flowers, streets. Engage in really smelling, tasting, touching—indulging the perceptive senses.

4) *Eventually, reorder your priorities, especially those that govern your use of time and energy.*

5) *Break through, somehow break through the enslavement of compulsive mechanical living to what I've come to call "tranquil aliveness."*

This "message" was delivered in part by my book *Compassion and Self Hate*, in which I describe a personal psychophilosophy that I believe can work against self-hate and depression. The last third of the book describes some of the inhumanities of the society we've constructed for ourselves and the destructive impact of that society upon us.

This book goes on from there, and its main purpose is to initiate a style of life, a personal philosophy that constructively runs counter to the most dangerous aspects of our current cultural structure. This, I believe, is possible only if we *reconcile* the various aspects of ourselves and also reconcile ourselves to the realities of the human condition. This makes "tranquil aliveness" and a mellow approach to living possible.

But can we change? Is the human mind capable of vast changes? In a work in progress called "The Kinetic Mind," which I've been writing for years, I describe the mind as an intricate chemical laboratory with a capacity to make virtually countless adaptations on demand. This means that human beings have an almost unlimited potential to construct diverse sociocultural patterns for behavior, because the brain, as a chemical laboratory, has the basic chemicals and the ability to transform them into an almost infinite number of combinations, which determine our behavior. While we are born with this chemistry, our behavior is also a function of choice and will and culture. Man, influenced by his internal chemistry, builds a society and then in turn is affected by that society. We have built a Frankenstein's monster in our chemistry laboratory—a monster of a culture that we must now destroy in order to enhance our possibilities for health; we must stand for our individual proclivities, health, and longevity against a society now geared to destroy us.

Our major weapon is the reconciled philosophy—or, in the current argot, the mellow philosophy. To participate in this philosophy involves a considerable readaptation. But human beings are capable of a great range of adaptations—even ones that might eventually drastically change the standards of society itself.

It is important, however, to realize that we seek no absolutes. *Relative* health, both on an individual and societal level, is what we are out for—for relativity is a corollary of being reconciled. Perfectionistic absolutes are the enemies of reconciliation.

2.

INNER PEACE AND OUR SOCIETY

ATTEMPTING A SUCCESSFUL bridge between biological reality and a psychotic cultural value system makes inner peace or a relative state of personal emotional equilibrium impossible. It's like trying to speak Chinese to a Frenchman. For this reason, books and theories that guarantee achievement in terms of the success value system—telling us how to "make it," how to "look out for number one," how to say no, how to win through intimidation—contribute to the destruction of inner peace. They tell us how to bond ourselves even more completely to the cultural values most antithetical to the human condition and its natural proclivities: they add to our continuing sense of failure and promote the mistaken notion that to be "unsuccessful" in terms of our materialist culture is to miss out on life entirely. Nor are tough-talking "success" programs the only enemies of reconciliation—there is a still more insidious school of thought that equates modern man's behavior with that of animals and pre-Paleolithic man. I believe that those who subscribe to this way of thinking destroy the reality of who we are here and now and contribute to

11

hopelessness by negating our capacity for peaceful living.

A New Theory of Relativity

Seeking to live by an antiquated competitive survival system can only widen the gap between the human beings we have become and the society we have created; it brings the individual still farther away from his real self, from inner peace and self-realization. Then what can work? Only struggle against cultural forces that would destroy inner peace and struggle for the development and realization of inner self. The idea is *not* to force the truly rich human self to impoverish itself in an attempt to live in a society poor in human values. The idea is to develop and to use our human substance, to struggle against and even change our impoverished society.

And it must be changed. A society that rejects all human assets and limitations, that preaches self-glorification and competitive strife, that forces us to see all that is human as alien to us rather than acceptable to us, is one that militates against and even destroys inner peace. Without inner peace, a stand for self, real self (as differentiated from glorified self), is almost impossible against a culture designed to promote inner turmoil, and we are doomed to live in a so-called age of anxiety.

What is this inner peace, and where does it come from? For me, it means a state of *relative well-being*, "feeling good," or "feeling together." Some people have felt this way so infrequently and so long ago that it is almost impossible for this to get beyond words and to recall—even momentarily—the moods and feelings characteristic of this mellow state. Listening to music, looking at paintings, or reading a wonderful book may sometimes help for a little while. But a major reevalua-

tion and struggle are usually necessary for any kind of
sustained state of well-being or "feeling together."
When I think of inner peace what comes to mind is a
long, lazy, languid, Huckleberry Finn kind of summer
afternoon, during which neither stimulation of any kind
nor boredom plays any significant role. But I'm sure
each of us has particular symbols—visual memories,
smells, words, incidents, books, people, songs—that
help bring back the kind of mood I'm talking about.
For many of us this kind of recollection, unfortunately,
must go all the way back to early childhood—and we
make the mistake of thinking that, in that far-off time,
we enjoyed *absolute* peace because our lives were so
much *simpler*.

But in life there are no absolutes. Indeed, the only *absolute* is death. To seek any absolutes, and this includes
absolute, uninterrupted inner peace, is to seek the impossible, and seeking the impossible makes for chronic
frustration, hopelessness, defeat, and resignation.

Relative inner peace is the antithesis of deadness.
Many of us have unwittingly become stimulation and
crisis addicts. And many of us feel "dead" unless we
feel very high and very low, so we engineer crises in
order to feel alive. Of course people suffering in this
way are terrified of inner peace, even relative inner
peace. I had one patient who produced successive crises
of increasing magnitude and destructiveness until he understood the mechanism involved. This man wrecked
several businesses and his marriage, and eventually
came close to death through hypertension before he
came for help. Not everyone creates anxiety of that
degree in order to feel alive, of course; but when you
rely on such stimulation, your moods and feelings not
only become increasingly difficult to attain and to
sustain but are in themselves relatively weak and superficial. Their blatant loudness passes for strength.

Relative inner peace on the other hand allows for
rich, deep feelings and moods; it awakens you to inner

and outer perceptions, however subtle they may be. It is as different from crisis stimulation as Mozart is from acid rock. It is the stuff of human depth and is the germinating soil for creative appreciation, living, and productivity. The joy that comes from perceiving the world we live in is at one and the same time a function of inner peace and a great contributor to inner peace, contributing to a constructive cycle.

Of course our moods will change, but *relative* inner peace will make difficult times and moods much easier—it strengthens us for harder times, helping us to accept life's realities and exigencies.

This is because when we repudiate false absolutes, we are at last able to see how good and bad can combine *together*. What about this word *together*—does it have anything to do with the common analytic term *integrated*? There is no such thing as a "simple" person. We are all "complex"—meaning that we all comprise different feelings, moods, yearnings, desires, or needs, many of which are often in conflict with each other. The same evolutionary development that freed us from inevitable competition with one another has also freed us from instinctual dictates, and has made a choice of behavior possible. But choice can be a heavy responsibility, especially when it dictates surrender of one or more desires in favor of one or more others. In an attempt to avoid inner conflict many of us avoid choice by avoiding desires and by deadening feelings generally. For example: I want to ask for a raise, but I am afraid to ask for it because I think the boss will deny me, so I make myself believe I don't care and I keep silent. In this way we inadvertently give up control of our total selves—as I gave up control over whether I got a raise or not—as we relegate parts of ourselves to unconsciousness and to individual autonomies. In other words, we fragment ourselves into separate selves, each sending mixed messages to the center of full consciousness. This makes for confusion and a sense of fragmentation and weakness.

Fragmentation and Integration

A good part of our lives is spent in attempts to put down unwanted feelings and conflict-producing aspects of ourselves through repression, dilution, or rationalization. This attempt to get rid of them and to be free of conflict destroys the possibility of choice, the most precious human gift. We can never actually get rid of aspects of ourselves that we don't want. The more we attempt to do so the more trouble they give us. When we try to idealize ourselves, to set up a glorious, impossible image of ourselves toward which we strive in order to feel "whole," the image eliminates all aspects of ourselves we see as less than ideal or as bad. Of course it doesn't work—the truth will out, and when it does, the resulting self-hatred just leads to further fragmentation as we pit our "good" self against our "bad" self.

Where does this need to fragment, to idealize, and to avoid choice come from? Largely from our culture, which in its idealization of an anti-human state of being attempts to make monstrous saints of us all. The truth is that we are *not* perfect: we are human, which means that we are afraid, limited, confused, mean, altruistic, generous, envious, sad, glad, energetic, tired, clear, understanding, angry, and many other things by turns and together. In this important context the word *together* alludes to accepting, as much as we can, all aspects of the humanity of our selves. This means living as real, alive people participating in the real, here-and-now world.

Picture a serene, deep, central stream of water into which all smaller branches pour water and which flows with peaceful strength. Now picture each branch overflowing in different directions, serving to deplete and to divert the central stream. The first picture is that of the integrated or "together" self—the *reconciled* self. The second is the fragmented self.

We are brought up and live in a society whose denial of human characteristics dictates fragmentation. This means all of us are relatively fragmented. But if we are to experience healthy change and growth, we must reconcile various aspects of ourselves, as much as possible, into a whole—we must recognize all aspects of our selves, and accept them, regardless of whether or not they fit cultural or self-imposed criteria for acceptance. Only this kind of self-growth can bring us alive inner peace—the antithesis of resignation and deadness, and the very essence of the mellow philosophy. And it is this alive inner peace that makes it possible for us to mend our fractured selves.

Our society encourages competition with self and others; it builds hierarchies of acceptance and importance in all areas of life. Religions preach humility but have their ecclesiastical pecking orders as well as their hierarchies based on various degrees of antihuman saintliness, purity, and martyrdom (all of them a kind of backhanded self-glorification). In medicine, some specialties are held in higher esteem than others, and hospitals, social status of particular patients, and practices become trappings of rank. In academia, rank of school and ranks within schools prevail. In games, maiming and sometimes even killing one's opponent, all under the guise of good sportsmanship, are almost as acceptable as in war. Wealth—evidence of the ancient ability to get to the jungle quarry sooner than the next fellow—determines prestige in just about all areas.

I am reminded of a man I know who asked me, "Without all this, what can we do? Where can we go? What purpose is there in life?" For him, life on a spontaneous basis, without the stimulation of imposed

striving, had no meaning. Over a lifetime he had exchanged real vitality born of inner peace and self-
realization for the synthetic aliveness of a pressured
existence imposed by a competitive, malignant, hierar-
chal society. He had already had one heart attack and
was justifiably afraid of another. He saw only two
possibilities. One was stress, and the other was deadness. He knew little or nothing of a third possibility: a
mellow approach to living and the vitality characteristic
of inner peace and reconciliation.

This man was not aware of how he had fragmented
himself in the service of a competitive society. He was
not aware of the chronic depletion he suffered as a
result of the constant war that took place between the
many fragments of his self. When splintering continues,
the various splinter groups battle each other for ascendancy and tear us apart. When parts of ourselves are at
war with other parts of ourselves, no class standing, no
amount of money, no kind of glory or popularity can
prevent misery, bad relationships, sickness, and death.
Tributaries become blocked before they can enter the
mainstream and the mainstream becomes dependent on
outside sources and gradually becomes dried up.

3.

RECONCILIATION— THE MAINSTREAM

COMPLEXITY CHARACTERIZES THE human condition: none of us is simple and none of us has sustained simple feelings. All of us have mixed and often diametrically opposed feelings, ideas, opinions, and thoughts about ourselves, other people, issues, and just about all things with which we come into contact. And our feelings do not remain static. They are in a constant state of flux, changing both in quality and intensity from time to time. To have conflicting feelings about issues, people, and the decisions that we make in our lives is one of the most common characteristics of human beings. *To be in conflict* (as this condition is usually called in psychoanalytic parlance) is characteristic of all of us.

Conflict—Conscious and Unconscious

The fact is that our parents nearly always have contrasting character structures—and their parents in turn had diverse characters. While there may be some genetic basis for character structure, I believe personality is in large part affected by role and position in the family. Unlike much simpler creatures who duplicate previous generations with almost absolute genetic and instinctual fidelity, *we* start out from life's earliest beginnings as recipients of both genetic and environmental influences of variable possibility.

One may almost say that we are born in conflict. As an example, let us imagine a child born to an expansive man and a self-effacing woman. The main characteristic of the expansive man is mastery—he works for admiration, prestige, and power. The self-effacing woman, on the other hand, sees herself as lovable, loving, and being loved—or at least being liked. Her husband sees himself as a leader and negotiates the world accordingly. She feels herself to be dependent and structures her behavior accordingly. (Of course neither one is *purely* expansive or self-effacing—everything is relative.) Now what about the child? The child adopts or inherits *both* attitudes—so he is in conflict. Eventually he adopts either self-effacement or mastery as his principal characteristic in an attempt to cope with the personality split that was provided by his initial connection with parents.

Like the child we have imagined, most of us, without being aware of it, are terrified of conflict and avoid it at all cost. But the cost of avoidance is high. Why do we avoid conflict? How do we avoid it? And, most pertinent to our discussion here, what is the cost?

Our culture ill prepares us for conflict. It sees human characteristics in black and white terms, or in terms of success or failure; good or bad; totally masculine or totally feminine; sick or healthy; rigidly imperfect or rigidly perfect; right or absolutely wrong; winning or losing; acceptably young or rejectably old. This kind of rigid approach to mixed feelings and issues makes for very sharp and strong divisions and for great intensity and polarization of feelings. This means that what might have been a diversification of feelings, which might have provided a richly interwoven internal fabric, has usually been converted into a psyche of sharp, divisive forces barely held together by all kinds of self-deluding stratagems. One young woman—let's call her Anne—frequently exhibited worry about her friends and colleagues; about their health, their schedules, their lives. Her solicitousness was accentuated in situations that might normally call for anger; if someone didn't appear for an appointment on time, Anne wouldn't show irritation but would worry that the other person might have met with an accident, or that she, Anne, had somehow not made the appointment correctly. Anything to avoid being angry. Her self-image as a loving, compassionate, "understanding" person would have been threatened by any displays of impatience, let alone outright anger, and her worrying, her obsessive scheduling and checking of times and places of meetings, her "concern" for friends and coworkers—all these were aids to repress her real feelings. When such stratagems fail, the usual result is explosive internal civil war, great pain in the form of anxiety and depression, and sometimes psychosis and inability to function at all. Anne began suffering increasingly severe bouts of stomach trouble and migraines; and she paid a larger price in terms of her ability to communicate honestly with other people—not to mention the time and energy she had to invest in concealing her true feelings and their origins.

Obviously, then, most of us unconsciously respond to mixed feelings, let alone to conflicting feelings and to major conflicts (such as conflicts between different aspects of our personalities), with trepidation and even terrible fright. Most of us will do anything to avoid confrontations. Why? Because what might have gone on as a pleasant consultation among various aspects of ourselves is automatically converted into internal tearing apart. One of my patients, a young man with a very active social life, had finally decided he wanted to get married and settle down; he had proposed to an extremely attractive girl with whom he felt very much in love, and they were going to be married in a month's time. He came to see me suffering from acute anxiety, and concomitant depression. What was wrong with him? Just when his fiancée was about to make him "the happiest man in the world" he felt terrified of being tied down. And he was confused and guilty over feeling this way. In an effort to avoid the awful tearing-apart anxiety of internal conflict, we resort to "defense mechanisms"—so well described by Karen Horney —which comprise every kind of machination we humans use in an effort to fool ourselves. These include rationalization, denial, hysteria, repression, projection (in which we blame others for our problems), dilution of feelings, illusions, delusions, avoidance, deadening— the list of unconscious internally-constructed contortions goes on and on.

The price we pay in order to convince ourselves that we are what we are not (an idealized, pride-invested version of ourselves) is enormous. We must invest most of our time and energy in this self-deluding process, and what little is left over is spent in complying with cultural standards. It is like trying to surf *against* the wave.

But depletion of energy and fatigue are only part of the price. In repressing what we *really* feel we cut ourselves off from ourselves, make aspects of ourselves unavailable for use, deaden ourselves so that we lose contact with our own feelings. This destroys spontaneity as well as creative possibilities. Even worse, it dilutes and sometimes obliterates a sense of real identity, the feeling of who we really are. This in turn makes for even sharper divisions, repressions, and inner deadening as well as malignant growth of still more illusions about the self and the human condition generally. In this process, our relationships with ourselves and others become increasingly wooden and attenuated as real aliveness, creativity, and the evolution and evolvement of self are surrendered in favor of spit-and-glue attempts to prevent conflict.

The Myth of Resolution

In keeping with cultural conditions that contributed to self-fragmentation in the first place, the demand is not one for *reconciliation* but unfortunately for *resolution*. Culture influences all of us—and I include psychotherapists—to want nothing short of complete resolution of conflict or conflicting feelings. We see resolution as the only way to restore internal harmony, aliveness, spontaneity, feeling of self, flexibility, the ability to make choices and decisions. But we must be very cautious here. Resolution is also an absolute. It connotes a static state of perfect solution, and it is the dream of a culture destructive to the complex human beings we are. Why would it be otherwise? A culture antithetical to human well-being would likely seek solutions to problems in ways that are also antithetical to human well-being.

The very use of the words *conflict* and *resolution* is revealing here. Conflict conveys feelings of antagonism. To borrow a term from physics, it is as if our emotions were *vectors*, or forces driving in different directions; if each emotional vector is loaded with passionate antagonism, we can readily see why fear of open confrontation exists and why fragmentation takes place. The implication of the process of resolution is that one vector will *win* and the other will *lose*. The further belief is that the losing vector will disappear and even die. Can these vectors be defused? Can emotional forces of different quality live in harmony within the self on an integrated basis? Can antagonism and conflict within the self be reduced and even minimized? Can we surrender the idea of repeatedly killing off one vector in favor of another and in so doing killing off parts of ourselves?

I believe that no conflict or diverse feeling is ever actually resolved. No choice or decision is ever complete in terms of the particular human being making that choice or decision. I believe that looking for attempts at "completeness"—efforts at "putting it away forever, now that the decision has been made"—are largely futile; they divert us from our mainstream, and make for fragmentation. But what about a different kind of approach, a process—and the idea of *process* is very important—of reconciliation?

Reconciliation is for me the process of living in relative peace with different aspects of ourselves as well as with other people. This is not an absolute or static condition that, once arrived at, provides a complete or permanent solution. The fact is that various aspects of self, various conflicting feelings and opinions will continue to be heard from. But if the true reconciling process is taking place, then they will be stated and heard in a different way. When you are reconciled with yourself, conflicting feelings and issues lack the compulsive rigidity and the tyrannical power characteristic of destructive conflict. When you stop investing such enormous pride in having it all, your choices and decisions are not life-and-death affairs. Nor do you feel it is a surrender each time one aspect of a conflicting situation takes precedence over another, so the feeling of splitting apart each time a choice is made is gone—as is the corresponding sense of loss. A man who realizes that he cannot be a playboy *and* a family man at the same time will be happier as his wedding approaches—the panic and depression disappear. Conflict and choice in the mellow framework are not approached with fear nor are there avoidance maneuvers resulting in continuing fragmentation.

Reconciliation encourages openness to all our feelings and desires, not just those to which we give priority at the moment. Does this mean that our decisions about our lives or our behavior must therefore change from minute to minute? No. A good decision lasts as long as it is good, but we do not have to cling to it slavishly if a reevaluation is in order and a change of decision is indicated. There is, however, always a price to pay— *always*—and only willingness to pay that price makes inner peace possible. No decision of any consequence can be made in our lives without some form of surrender. Each choice entails exchanging one status quo for another. Only one condition can prevail at a time; therefore we must pay the price of giving up one condition or set of circumstances in order to sustain another. What we choose to do in a given situation depends on our establishing a *hierarchy of priorities*. This means establishing a scale of real importance: if we want to take a trip to Europe, but we also want to remodel the kitchen in our house, we must understand that we don't have enough money to afford both, and we must decide which is more important to us. If a temporary respite, a change of scene, a true holiday is more necessary to us, obviously we choose the trip since (under those circumstances) we realize that we can perfectly well live with the kitchen the way it is for another year.

This is the stuff of reconciliation, not resolution. It is a process in which we become reconciled not only with ourselves, but to other people, the human condition, and the world. To become healers of fractures and gentle handlers of self, rather than demolition experts and executioners and morticians, entails struggle with cultural demands and confusions that would have it otherwise. This is similar to the struggle we engage in when we attempt to give up our neuroses. Our neurotic defense systems are intimately connected with the demands and values of the society we live in—each after all gives birth to the other and continues to feed the other—and the patient who enters psychoanalysis does more than struggle to free himself from the onslaught of unconscious drives and fragmenting forces. He does more than reveal to himself hitherto hidden aspects of himself so that he may choose which to give priority at a given moment. He removes himself from being an automaton, a willy-nilly bit of flotsam that goes here or there as the cultural value system dictates. He struggles to become a spontaneous individual, not a compliant slave. This does not mean that his life falls unwaveringly into line with his purpose, or that he is "in command"—this is *not* the stuff of soldiery, the military and war and death. This is the stuff of humanity, the extension and growth of still further humanity and life, and real aliveness.

In resolution, we resolve; and of course most resolutions are broken. However much we desire to kill off feelings that might have led to decisions other than those we made—decisions based on other vectors—they simply refuse to die. This is further evidence of the aliveness of human protoplasm and the tenacity with which we cling to all aspects and evidence of life and our alive selves.

In reconciliation we seek no final solution, no perfect tranquillity, no absolute harmony. We are seeking to have a relatively fair working arrangement with the various aspects of ourselves and with the world we live in. We know that reconciliation is an ongoing process and that various tributary feelings must and will continue to be heard from so that they can enter the mainstream.

In reconciliation we remain at peace and in friendship with vectors that do not lead to decisions and actions. We expect and accept yearnings that currently cannot be filled as we try to accept all realities of life. In short we refuse to close ourselves off to ourselves in response to either internal or external pressures. We remain open people, open both to inner and outer perceptions in continuing loyalty to the reconciling process of mainstream living, a process that not only integrates and strengthens the self but in so doing makes real spontaneity and choice possible.

It is only through this process of reconciliation with ourselves that we can really achieve inner peace. For in the state of harassment in which a great many of us habitually live we often forget or neglect situations—places, people, activities—that give us peaceful pleasure. The question we can periodically ask ourselves is, *What gives us peaceful pleasure?* Relative to this question obviously there are other ones, too. Have we neglected this question for too long? Why? What can we do about it? Is it time to reassess our priorities? Have we lost touch with what gives us pleasure? If the last is true, perhaps a struggle is necessary in order once again, or for the first time, to put us in touch with and to extend pleasurable areas in our lives.

4.

EASY ALIVENESS, STRUGGLE, AND SELF-REALIZATION

BY "EASY ALIVENESS," I mean an easygoing aliveness, in which comfort or peace is infinitely more important than excitement. But peace in no way connotes lifelessness or lack of vitality. On the contrary, easy aliveness results from self-awareness, and is the germinating medium of both spontaneity and creative production. It may seem paradoxical for me to say it cannot be achieved without struggle—but we must be careful here in our understanding both of the condition and of the terms I've been using.

Struggle versus Suffering

There is a vast difference from my point of view between struggling and suffering. Suffering, when it is self-imposed, is nearly always the result of forces that remain at least partially unconscious. A man who works an eighteen-hour day in order (so he thinks) to provide for his family is not struggling. He is suffering. He isn't providing for his family, he is destroying it—he has no time to get to know his children or to share little intimacies with his wife, he cannot grow or change with them, or enjoy them. He feels that his overwork, his harassed commuting, and his overstuffed briefcase are suffered for the sake of his family—but they are really suffered for martyrdom, and the self-glorification he derives from it. One cannot strive for martyrdom and conquest at the same time and succeed. Glory itself is fleeting and empty. The quest results in further repression, more unconscious labyrinth-like devices, and still more fragmentation. Suffering occurs as the result of martyrdom, but more important, it occurs as a result of the emptiness and hopelessness that ensue each time there is either a failure or a success in terms of self-glorification goals.

Our society equates happiness with impressing other people—either with our power or prestige or with our purity, self-sacrifice, perfect love, or saintliness. Some of us come to believe that we haven't achieved enough and confuse overachieving or suffering with struggling. Our overworked family man has come to believe that he isn't working hard enough; he isn't making big enough deals, and he drives himself to make the Enormous Deal that will somehow fulfill him—thereby robbing himself still further. The joys of close family life, of the conviviality of friends continue to elude him.

If he *stopped* suffering, and asked himself, "What am I missing?", if he put up a struggle against what society has taught him to expect of himself, he might be able to stop this cycle of suffering.

Struggling involves loyalty to the whole self rather than to its parts. Peace is more important than stimulation and excitement. Self-realization is more important than any kind of external confirmation of self through admiration, money, position in any kind of hierarchy, rewards, promotions, and the like. Struggling in this context always refers to the struggle for healthy change and growth. This kind of change and growth is the antithesis of ruthless (to the self) self-aggrandizement. We are involved here not in a search for glory but in a search for *authenticity*. Authenticity springs from real feelings, real aliveness, real spontaneity. These realities are the opposite of obsessive compulsions, and achieving them necessitates a struggle against participation in the competitive rat race.

But this struggle need not be a painful one, and it does not seek to inflict pain on others. Struggle in this process is similar to the struggle the true scholar engages in as he unravels mysteries of the universe and studies what interests him for his own satisfaction and personal enrichment. I am reminded of the ecstasy the true talmudic student experiences as he struggles to learn more about the human condition. He never feels that he will *attain* it—spontaneity cannot be captured, pinned down, or made to stand still. When a river is made to stand still it becomes a stagnant pond. It is no longer a river. The struggle itself is the aliveness we seek; it *is* the spontaneity and it is always in process. It is never over, but lasts all of our lives, because as Karen Horney pointed out, we are capable of healthy change and growth all of our lives.

Change and Growth

Change and growth are a process. They can be measured not in static terms, but by the extent to which we find ourselves involved in the process of self-realization.

The term self-realization has always bothered me because it is too vague. But as I use it, it describes the process of using energy for the evolution of the real self as opposed to the pseudo-self, the idealized image of yourself that society pressures you to create. It is a *dynamic* process, not a static one, and therefore it can be measured only in relative terms. These are the basic ingredients of change and growth:

1) *The range and depth of feelings.* Of course you cannot gauge your feelings if you aren't in touch with them—with your own tastes, preferences, or opinions. Many people start treatment in psychoanalysis unaware of the extent to which they are alienated from feelings. They have led lives comprised of muted and deadened feelings for years; and sometimes this emotional deadness anesthetizes them physically. Sometimes the first evidence of progress in awakening feelings is pain: gastritis, lower back ache, or something similar. Of course they go on to feel much more—the warmth of the sun on their faces, the exhilaration of a long walk, the tenderness conveyed by a wife's smile, warmth toward a loved one—and anesthetic mechanical living gives way to alive spontaneity.

2) *Increasing interest and receptivity in terms of perception.* This means actually enjoying seeing, smelling, touching, and hearing more and more. I remember my own first sense of increased perception through touch, after I had been in treatment for a year and a half. I had no idea of the range of sensitivity that was possible with my hands and fingertips. More and more I enjoy the feel of different fabrics—roughly woven cloth, silk, and satin; the feel of cold, warm, and hot water; the feel of clay, granite, and the various curves and lines of statues, hair, cheeks, a baby's nose, ears, and hands.

Some time ago I suffered a relatively severe corneal abrasion. This necessitated a very large dressing and bandage that covered almost half my face and head. This went on for two weeks. During this period of time, five of my patients (they did not lie on the couch; they sat facing me) whom I saw nearly every day said nothing. They never noticed. A few years later—after these same patients had been in therapy with me for some time—I had a small skin lesion removed from my face, which required a minute Band-Aid. This time they all saw it immediately and were obviously concerned about my well-being.

3) *Reconciliation of self with self*. This means becoming more and more aware of all aspects of our selves, no matter how ambivalent or contradictory, as contributors to a rich human fabric.

4) *Reconciliation to reality*. We must see and negotiate the world and the people in it with ever-growing reality, as illusions are increasingly dissipated and delusions surrendered. We must know what is possible and impossible. This reconciliation also includes standing up for our own values in the face of society's demands on us.

5) *Increased knowledge of one's own assets and limitations, and the growth of one's own philosophy of life*. The latter largely means realistic cognizance of what is and isn't important to us in life; taking our selves seriously and using our time and energy in the service of self-realization rather than any kind of culturally esteemed pseudo-self-aggrandizement.

Activity that is used for self-idealizing or that fails to take the self seriously represents a waste of time and energy. Both time and energy are limited by our mortality, alas—which is not to suggest that we should impose the pressure of timetables or workloads on ourselves (I shall say more about that later on) any more than it is to say that pleasurable pursuits waste time or energy. But energy and time thrown away, against our real desires and proclivities, because society says we must do so— that is a waste. I think of countless anesthetic hours spent before television sets; huge parties in which no real contact between people takes place. The real test is how we feel afterward. Some activities make us feel richer in ourselves. Others leave us feeling impoverished and demoralized.

Increasing knowledge of one's own assets and limitations is difficult and involves considerable struggle. It is as hard for the self-effacing person to appreciate personal assets as it is for the expansive person to assess his limitations. It is equally hard for the reserved, detached person to appreciate either assets or limitations, his own or others, in terms of relating to other people.

6) *Increasing love of yourself, others, and the human condition in general*. This is a measurement of your hatred—or lack of it—of human characteristics and limitations; of particular people and groups of people; and of yourself. It involves a stand against prejudice engendered by a sick culture against any group or person: ethnic groups, the young, the old, the infirm, the intellectuals, the poor, the rich, or whomever.

Love of self and others does not preclude breaking destructive relationships—in fact one cannot love one's self without being free to do just that, to sever relationships that depress, deplete, and demoralize.

Love here does not refer to an idealized form of storybook ecstasy or to a melding of selves into a two-headed monster. On the contrary, *real* love, of self and others, necessitates respect for individual selves and a helpful exchange between two real and separate human beings. In this connection I'd like to say two things about psychotherapy. First, if the therapist is not being helped and advancing his own integration in helping the patient, the therapy is either anti-therapeutic or very superficial indeed. Second, the most effective therapy for an individual who hates himself is to love him, to desire to help him, and to care. This more than anything else is effective in starting his own self-loving machinery going again.

In real self-love, as differentiated from narcissistic preoccupation with self, interest in others increases.

Healthy self-love involves loving *all* of oneself. This means that a really self-loving individual is one who has learned the lesson of compassion for himself and is continuing to learn it. If he looks back at any aspect of his life, he looks back with understanding—not ridicule or embarrassment or hatred. Such self-love is evidence of integration and in a way is even synonymous with it. This is so because as we love aspects of ourselves we bring them together rather than trying to keep them apart. Some people experience the apart feelings rather concretely and in a frightening way, called in psychiatry a disassociative reaction. In this condition they feel as if they are outside or apart from themselves, looking at themselves in a panicked state of loss of identity. We all do this on a subtler level when one part of us stands aside and judges another part pejoratively. Harsh judgments are not the stuff of love, and especially not of helping and integrating love.

7) *Creativity*. The active process of being creative is a superb measuring rod of one's total engagement in self-realization. I use the term creative in the broadest sense to include *all* production that seeks to tap inner resources and to bring natural proclivities to realization and fruition. Creative enterprise has the therapeutic effect of bringing the self together as it employs all nuances and aspects of self. The more serious the creative enterprise is, that is, the more involved the creator is in the work, the more aspects of self and experiences of personal history will be used making this binding more secure.

Nearly all neurotic symptoms or suffering can be traced back to neglect of one of these seven areas of change and growth. Self-hate, depressions, and disturbed relationships with others indicate lack of struggle for increasing love of self and others (6). Difficulties stemming from poor perception of self, and leading to thwarted expectations, indicate lack of work on perception (2).

Struggle is, then, the antithesis of neurotic suffering, and is in fact the antidote and cure for neurotic pain. It is also the antithesis of resigned stagnation and obsessive compulsive rigidity. It best takes place in a state of relative peace, even as it produces peace and mending within the self. The quest for true self-realization is the antithesis of competition or the building of hierarchical status relative to others. It is marked by absence of vindictive triumph and aggression, and its true hallmark relative to other people is cooperation. Of course, how we relate to others is crucial to the philosophy we follow and describes an all-important link between ourselves and our society.

5.

COMPETITION, COOPERATION, AND LOVE

In *Compassion and Self Hate* I wrote about how competition is a form of self-hate and how our culture has come to believe that competition "brings out the best" in people. I still believe that it brings out the worst. It is intimately linked to envy, jealousy, and paranoia, and blocks evolvement and development of self. It ultimately has a depleting and deadening effect on self as its unrelenting demands are met and self-realizing needs are ignored.

Competitive Self-Hate

In competition, the focus of one's life is essentially outside one's self. The use of our time and energy is determined by our competitors rather than by our own selves and our own real needs. This weakens our own sense of identity, and to compensate for this ever-increasing feeling of emptiness and vulnerability we compete still more, completing a self-depleting cycle. When enough depletion takes place to preclude further "successful" competition, we feel hopeless and futile and our lives seem purposeless.

Despite talk about good sportsmanship, competition is totally incompatible with the kind of easy aliveness that is the aim of this book. It flourishes in an atmosphere of high stimulation (tennis players' insistence on being "psyched up" reminds me of my patient who could only thrive on crisis) and vindictive triumph. Its rewards and goals are immediate and short-lived, and self-glorification guarantees virtual exclusion of self-realization. It destroys our inner sense of autonomy and stability and is also destructive to outside relationships and to real communication. Competitive friction is inimical to kindness, and without kindness a self-enriching philosophy is impossible. Despite protestations and reassurances about "friendly competition," antagonists are not friendly. The "feeling good" that competitors say comes from competition is based on someone else's feeling bad. And this "feeling good" doesn't last because it is based on putting the next fellow down rather than on a sustained strengthening of yourself through self-realization. So competition becomes addictive.

Competition is a residual of a primitive past, and it is *not* a genetic residual. It is passed on to us through training in our society from generation to generation. This training starts early and can usually be seen in very early sibling rivalry. I do not believe that rivalry among children of the same family is instinctual. I believe that it is engendered by parents who themselves were victims of victims: they may convey the competitive motif blatantly or so subtly that it is not readily perceived. They themselves are caught in the same trap—they spend enormous time and energy getting ahead of the Joneses. Small wonder so many children are pressured into Little League or equivalent competitive structures—all with rationalization that this will promote their self-development, well-being, and health. Actually these activities and organizations nearly always serve as vicarious vehicles designed to satisfy *parental* craving for competitive success. People brought up in this way feel lost if they are suddenly thrust into a situation of low competitive tension. They exist to compete and they've lost their *raison d'être*, so they invent hierarchies and games to provide the stimulation they need to "keep the motor running," even if these inventions are ultimately destructive to inner peace and personal health.

I am reminded of my own medical school experience in Lausanne, Switzerland. I was part of a group of about eighty Americans studying at the medical faculty of the university at that time. The system was non-competitive. People who were qualified were accepted into the school. These consisted of people who received passing grades in the required premedical or foundation courses. Two series of examinations—one in the basic sciences one and one half years after admission, and the other after studies were completed—determined qualification for graduation. Students were allowed to postpone these examinations as long as they felt was necessary. To pass, students were required to demonstrate adequate knowledge of the material. The atmosphere was totally benevolent and without the presence of any coercion or intimidation whatsoever. There was no "curve" and students were not graded relative to each other.

The Swiss students exhibited great camaraderie among themselves, helped each other, and for the most part demonstrated great proficiency in grasping and integrating the material. There were no "tricks" whatsoever, no surprise quizzes or exams. Indeed there were no examinations at all, other than the two sets of standardized government exams. Requirements for passing the examinations were well defined for everyone. Instruction was superb.

We Americans arrived as graduates of a highly competitive system. Indeed, many of us arrived as refugee victims of that system. We were all qualified to attend medical school inasmuch as all of us had satisfactorily completed bachelor degrees in the premedical courses necessary for medical school. Some of us had fair grades in premedical courses, some good grades, and some excellent. None of us had been admitted to an American medical school. Some had been excluded because of the Jewish quota quite prevalent in our own country at that time; some because we had gone to the "wrong schools" (excellent schools academically but not held in high esteem socially or politically—these were usually the city colleges of New York); some of us for receiving good but not perfect grades; and some of us for all three reasons.

By the time we arrived in Switzerland our paranoia ran high. I suppose we suffered a kind of culture shock. Few of us could believe that medical school could be such a straightforward, noncompetitive activity, and that we would be required to learn only the material we were told to learn. (Some of us remembered too well taking competitive examinations that contained questions on the most abstruse reading, some of it "non-required.")

Stimulation addicts like ourselves found little motivation in the Swiss system—so we formed competitive cliques. Some people convinced themselves and others that the Swiss professors were tricky and that the two sets of exams could never be passed. Others stated that the school was not good, below standard, and that it would never be recognized in the United States. (This belief persisted, despite the fact that the school had been in existence for hundreds of years and was superb in all respects.) People kept secret from each other the ready availability of course notebooks. Bets were made as to who would and who would not get through. Scouts were secretly sent from various cliques to see if other European schools were better. People tried to convince other people that they would never get through and should return home. There was much gossip about absences from classes and who was and who wasn't dedicated to medical school and his chosen field. Former friends who came to Switzerland together stopped talking to each other because they now saw each other as competitors.

The Swiss went on as they always did. The Americans did also. They had re-created American competition in Switzerland. Some of them became so panicked and depressed that they packed up and went home, giving up their life's desire forever. Some adjusted to the benevolent society they found themselves in and became good doctors. But even now, after some thirty years, one of my former Lausanne classmates still feels he has to say that the Swiss medical schools were particularly tough to get through—he must exaggerate a sense of accomplishment by exaggerating the difficulty or if necessary inventing it. And after I graduated from medical school I heard that several suicides had occurred among students who came after me. I wondered about the role hysterical competition had played in these tragedies.

When my son Jeff, now an M.D. and a psychiatrist, was taking a microbiology examination in premed school, he realized that most of the students were making sure that the microscopes they had used were out of focus before passing on to succeeding specimens—this to make it more difficult for their "colleagues" taking the exam. What effect can this kind of cutthroat competition to get into medical school, and to stay there, have on our future medical practitioners?

Competition damages people other than students. It provides a stressful, isolating, and paranoid atmosphere that is the very antithesis of peace of mind. Competitive strivings are not felt directly or blatantly. They do not occur solely when we are locked in antagonistic embrace with adversaries—we have, after all, come a considerable distance from the dinosaurs. But the subtle influence of competitive standards to be met and our consciousness of how the next guy is doing—in terms of earnings, position, accomplishments, notoriety, possessions, or whatever—work their subtle and not-so-subtle corrosive effects. They provide constant pressure and undermine our efforts to build a self-realizing value system. This means that we are more involved with how the next fellow is doing than with knowing what *we* really want to do. We are more concerned with how *they* feel about us than how we feel.

Competition also contributes to a mood of paranoia. Since anyone and everyone can be a potential or actual competitor, suspiciousness reigns supreme and openness is viewed with contempt. This makes it very difficult to accept and to feel the nourishing effects of give-and-take and often makes much-needed help from others impossible to accept. Our culture in large measure has made this paranoid closure to nourishment from others a virtue, especially a masculine virtue, often rationalized by ideas about independence and self-reliance. Independence and self-reliance are valuable assets but often they are actually cover-ups of fear of other people and are functions of sick pride invested in isolation and rejection of other people's much-needed help.

Competition in this way also has a powerful fragmenting effect: it causes us to be preoccupied with fragmented single areas rather than with integration and wholeness. Competitors almost inevitably become specialists, limiting the area of their endeavors and concentrating all their energy in the pursuit of one goal in order to beat the competition. Thus, the big "successes" in our culture are usually successful in their given areas but fail in all others.

I am reminded of somebody I know who joined a neighborhood orchestra some years ago. The orchestra was formed for mutual enjoyment and it had a wonderfully therapeutic effect for years. The members shared much camaraderie and music. They were "not the greatest players" in the world but this in no way diluted their pleasure. Then, about a year ago, someone mentioned "a hot young conductor" who was looking for an orchestra. The young man shortly afterward became the leader of the orchestra my friend had joined. It improved markedly and even gave well-attended concerts in some of the best halls around the city. But a change had taken place. The young conductor now spoke of who was and who wasn't good for the orchestra. He spoke of "getting things done perfectly." He also spoke of bringing in people who were "more professional." Several months after his arrival, sociability had just about ceased, and meetings had become pure work sessions. The conductor established a hierarchy of qualifications but soon this was not enough. He decided to hold auditions. Interestingly, no one thought of getting rid of the conductor. By this time the orchestra members were all caught up in the competitive schema and some members claimed that they enjoyed the stimulation of status achievement. Recently, several members were dropped. The rest of the orchestra acquiesced in these dismissals. A few of the dropped musicians were people in their seventies who had been with the orchestra for years. One man wept and said that the one remaining joy in his life was gone. The conductor brought in accomplished young musicians and the orchestra became "sharp enough" to play in paid, well-attended, very prestigious concerts. The person who told me the story said it was no longer the same. "Everyone is uptight, worried, and no longer friendly." Capitulation to competitive cultural sickness had taken place. My friend was heartsick and wondered if he would continue playing much longer.

Competition and Love

Competition is a great disturber of inner peace. I mean this. Competition stands in the way of our natural human proclivity for wanting, needing, and having open and loving intercourse with other people. How can we be open if we've come to believe that others are potential enemies? But, if we're at all healthy, we still want open, loving, cooperative, nourishing relationships with others—even as we receive messages to the contrary from a disturbed society.

A middle-aged patient of mine, a senior editor at a large publishing house, had a daughter in her late twenties who had many assets—beauty, intelligence, and a flourishing career as a television producer. She surpassed her mother in areas that both considered of vital importance; at twenty-eight, she was already an executive at her network. The daughter was "an achiever" because, as her mother said, "all the women in our family are achievers." In other words, each generation of women in the family had pressured the next generation into "achievement." As long as the daughter—call her Nancy—had been dependent on her mother, they had had a peaceful and supportive relationship; but soon after Nancy got her promotion she and her mother began to have arguments. The mother, Alice, came to see me feeling very upset and estranged from Nancy. "I just never see her anymore," she told me, but when asked at what point the relationship had become strained she couldn't answer. She did not realize how the emphasis on "achievement" in her family had undermined her feelings for her daughter. Such conflict shows up in husband/wife, parent/child, and sibling relationships in which there are great disturbances as attempts are made to reconcile open, loving feelings with competitive, suspicious feelings imposed over a lifetime.

Unfortunately our competitive culture produces very little trust, either in ourselves or in others. Real trust in others is virtually impossible when nearly all other people are seen as adversaries. Some spouses attempt to build bridges across such malignant feelings of distrust by actual possession of their mates. They come to see husbands and wives as extensions of themselves rather than as separate human beings, and this makes stifling what could be a fruitful relationship: jealousy and envy corrode both internal peace and peace between relating partners. Trust is of course a primary ingredient in openly relating with ourselves and with others and in establishing both inner peace and peace with each other.

True Love and Anti-Love

Even as our society pushes us into the mutual hatred of competition, it idealizes love. Songs, TV, movies, and word-of-mouth bombard us with myths of total, un-compromising, never-having-to-say-you-are-sorry, un-able-to-live-without-you love. Actually, this version of love and adult relationships is in keeping with a society that largely sees things in extremes and abhors so many real aspects of the human condition. Of course we human beings need to relate and to communicate, but we are *separate* entities with individual needs and appetites. To adapt to each other entails considerable struggle, despite the chemistry that may attract and bind us. When we forget this and idealize love, we court inevitable disappointment, self-hate, and depreciation of the kind of relatedness we human beings are really capable of.

I call this mythologized love *anti-love*, because it is the antithesis of the warm feelings we have for other human beings for whom we care. Anti-love is actually an extension of the self-idealizing process and has as its underpinnings morbid dependency needs, the need to absorb and to be absorbed, and the need to worship and to be worshiped. In anti-love the lover projects his own idealized self onto the loved object and in so doing obliterates any real interest in or involvement with the actual person he claims to love. This precludes respect for the partner's integrity as a person and denies the partner's individual proclivities, talents, or limitations —as when a man whose wife hates traveling persistently arranges cruise vacations for the two of them because "I know she's just dying to get away." On the deepest level this is an attempt by the fragmented person to extend a weak self, much as an amoeba extends a pseudopod to engulf food, and to produce synthetic strength. This kind of attempt to satisfy dependency is often seen between parents and children (the parents want their children to have everything they themselves didn't) and causes disturbed relationships as well as further fragmentation.

Anti-love also takes place between mutually exploitative adult partners who may spend many years in each other's physical presence without being together or really getting to know each other at all. Each has been engaged in an attempt to absorb the other, or has used the other as a relatively blank screen on which to project his or her own image. For example, how many couples consistently give one another presents that each returns—presents that were bought for the *giver*, not the receiver. This kind of relationship is certainly narcissistic; we might even say it is autistic, meaning the energy and time are largely used in the service of compulsive preoccupation with the sickest aspects of unrealistic self. Is it any wonder that—since it narcotizes away all other feelings and thoughts, especially those involving realities of living in the real world—anti-love is often characterized by selfish obsessive possessiveness, jealousy, envy, disappointment, thwarted expectations, rage, and depression? This is not the stuff of love. Then what is love?

Of course I do not deny the existence or importance of aesthetic or physical attraction between people. I've listed the perceptions of the senses as one of the dynamics of self-realization, and these sensual perceptions certainly include physical relationships and the expression of feelings through sexual encounter.

But what about love between people on the broadest level? What about cooperation, caring, kindness, and help? These are, to me, the essence of love, and they are supplemented by the desire to share feelings and thoughts. This kind of love is not a storybook idealization or a romantic notion on my part; cooperative *relat-*

ing is essential for the survival and well-being of the communicating, social creatures we are. Cooperation, not competition, brings out the best in us. Love, or cooperative relating, involves knowing and helping somebody else. This involves a *real* mutual exchange, a true enriching process, virtually antithetical to society's aberrant vision of love.

Cooperation is marked by respect and—even more than respect—*love* of the integrity (wholeness) and individuality of the other person. This is the antithesis of vicarious living through the other person. Love is marked by a healthy desire to know another. This desire takes the form of warm, friendly, noncompetitive curiosity about who and what the other person *is*, quite apart from who we ourselves are. This interest in who the other person really is brings satisfaction and joy much as knowledge brings joy to the scholar, for its own sake and as a contribution to one's own humanity. In this kind of openness to knowing, there is no interest in comparisons, in judgments, in goods or in bads. This is the sort of accepting affection that can often be seen in relationships between parents and very young babies, but unfortunately, the relationship often gets muddied by odious comparisons and competitions as the baby grows up and the parents become pressured by societal influences. They forget that *to know* each other involves knowing each other's feelings, thoughts, and values.

Alexander Reed Martin, a very wise psychoanalyst of the American Institute for Psychoanalysis, published a paper on reassurance some years ago, in which he said that there is little that is as reassuring to a patient as a correct interpretation. Dr. Martin means that a therapist, in making a correct interpretation, adequately demonstrates to the patient his own comprehension of what the patient is feeling. I've come to call this kind of deeper-than-intellectual knowing *feel knowing*. When it passes between us, it provides potent help because it adequately demonstrates the existence of a communicating bridge of humanity and caring; this bridge, which transcends our separate skins and selves, can't fail to generate hope and encouragement. And the more we know about a person the more we can help. Mellow, reconciling, and loving relating involves nonjudgmental, nonmoralizing help, similar to the help the professional psychoanalyst gives to his patient. The motive is, after all, not to impose one's own imprint, but rather to help the other person to experience and develop his or her own individuality.

Now why is this kind of helping such a powerful therapeutic, integrating instrument for the helpers? In competition and anti-love we actually project the idealization of ourselves on to another person and then compete with that projection of self. Bill, a young professor of social history, felt that he was a supportive husband: he constantly encouraged his wife, Betty, to continue graduate work and to write and publish, because, as he said, he didn't want her to stop trying to make something of herself after their marriage. Betty went on to receive a doctorate in anthropology and she has now published several well-received papers; but she laughingly confesses that without Bill around to push her she would never have gotten where she is. She is compliant and easygoing, and would have been just as happy if she were "achieving" less. Interestingly, Bill's and Betty's relationship has become increasingly disturbed as Betty achieves more and more. Although all their friends say they envy Betty for having such a supportive husband, Bill is becoming progressively unhappier as Betty succeeds—yet still he "encourages" her to go after bigger and better prizes. Bill is really using Betty vicariously, and at the same time resents the threat she poses to his position as the "professional" in the family; additionally, he feels increasing pressure to surpass her newly won position. Thus Bill, like many of us, is competing with himself and contributing to the process of suffering rather than struggling.

Helping others is the substance of love. In helping others we call upon ourselves to unify and tap all of our resources in order to give of ourselves to another person. Giving makes us whole, reconciled, integrated. I believe that no other human activity has an equally reconciling effect. Help comes in many forms; the artist helps with his paintings, the musician with his music, and so on. The gift of any service represents a kind of reconciliation, but close-up, direct, cooperating, and loving help, the help that involves real open knowing, truly aids the giver in the reconciliation of his own diverse experiences and feelings, and in his own creativity, perception, and resourcefulness generally.

Kindness is not an aberration or a pretense. I believe that it is a natural and spontaneous inclination of people to be kind to each other. This is made especially easy for members of our species because of our ability to identify and to empathize with each other. Kindness is the foundation of cooperation, and as intelligent creatures, we know that survival is possible only with cooperation.

What do I mean by kindness? I see kindness largely as an appreciation of *each other's* assets, yearnings, needs, tastes, individual proclivities, fallibilities, limits, problems, vulnerabilities, and sensibilities. Kindness includes acceptance of differences—*without* equivocations or conditions. In our society kindness is often looked upon as an aberration and as a block and potential threat to personal success. Kindness is often equated with foolishness; kind people are referred to as "do-gooders," or "bleeding hearts." Cruelty, on the other hand, which I regard as truly inhuman, is often held in high regard and seen as being practical, strong, part of "getting ahead." I am not talking about blatant sadistic manipulation. Simply to disregard human sensibilities, needs, or frailties is to be cruel. That cruelty is so commonly found and admired in our society is not unexpected, considering the paranoid competitive framework in which we find ourselves.

But cruelty is not only destructive to relationships. It also prevents an exercise of our own self-realizing processes and produces an inner drying up and shrinkage. This is not a surface phenomenon and may not be noticeable immediately, but it has its repercussions throughout one's life, especially in close relationships. You cannot operate as a noncaring, mind-your-own-business, cruel, and competitive person all day and then turn on cooperative machinery when you get home to mate and children. When Kenneth comes home from the office he tries to flip the switch to sweetness and gentleness—but he's only putting on an act. His performance is wooden, mechanical, and studied, and its phony quality is fast picked up by those around him. His children feel no real warmth or affection, and so instead of sitting around to chat with him about the day's events, they quickly vanish to their rooms. Kenneth is depriving himself of spontaneity and real depth of feeling. Kenneth would be better off if he came home still fuming about the inadequate estimate someone gave him at the office—or even if he displaced that same rage and used it against his family. At least that would clear the air and allow other feelings—of warmth and tenderness—to emerge. Either way, of course, he pays a price; but one is clearly more costly than the other.

I think of cruelty exercised here, and especially in Japan, on children hardly out of infancy who are forced to compete for the "right nursery schools." In Japan "failure" of four-year-olds to gain admission often determines their "class" standing for a lifetime. This application of cruelty, an extension of much other cruel, competitive, cultural activity, starts the self-shrinkage process going very early in life and must have dire consequences—poor self-esteem, anxiety, depression, even suicide—later on.

But let me describe quite a different kind of experience, one that I mentioned briefly elsewhere. Some years ago I was in charge of a large number of patients hospitalized in a huge public institution. Personnel were badly lacking and care was at best limited and sometimes nonexistent. There was one patient, Mary, who

was severely depressed and who felt completely
hopeless. She hardly ate, talked, or moved. I tried to get
her to walk about the ward and to talk but my efforts
for the most part were of no avail. She spent day after
day sitting in one spot, staring at the wall, mute and
barely eating. But I was able to make contact with her.
She didn't respond to me verbally but she did eat a little
bit when I sat nearby and talked to her. Finally, after
several weeks of sitting with her and talking, I told her
to look around at the other patients. I said that it was
important that she realize that although she was very
depressed, other patients were much sicker than she was
and needed help, which for the most part was not
available.

This was true. Most of the people were totally out of
contact. No words could reach them. Many walked
about actively hallucinating, completely cut off from
the world around them. Several had become totally
disoriented, nonverbal automatons. Some never ate
unless spoon-fed and a few had to be fed through
stomach tubes. Mary looked around and nodded her
head in agreement: indeed, other people were sicker and
in greater need than she. I told her that we needed her
help, that she must pick out one patient and devote herself to helping that one patient every day. I took her
hand and we went from person to person in the ward,
and I described the problems of each of them as we
came to them. She didn't make an active choice. She
was too depressed to do that. But I finally said, "How
about this lady?" and she nodded in consent. The
woman we picked for her to help—Rose—was quite old
and totally disoriented. She needed *total* care, much as
an infant does. This included feeding, washing, toilet
care—everything. Mary started gradually to take care of
her "patient," Rose. She started by sitting with her. By
the second day she took Rose's hand several times a day
and walked her around the ward. After a few days she
took over the attendants' job and fed her.

In a week Mary spoke to Rose and demonstrated a

considerable improvement in her own appetite. She continued to speak to Rose more and more and in the following weeks spoke to me also. Rose had suffered considerable organic damage due to advanced cerebral arteriosclerosis, but she perked up a little bit too, although her general orientation did not improve and she remained confused and helpless. But Mary improved enough to go home and to continue psychotherapy on an outpatient basis. Her own regenerative forces had become activated by involvement in the process of helping a fellow human being.

On several occasions when I too have been quite depressed, I have been able to help myself and to feel better by helping people who were feeling even worse. Being a doctor is no small privilege. There are of course times in therapy when the therapist doesn't help, and when the patient does not improve. Is it possible that at least in some of these cases the therapist has not loved the patient enough? I ask this question because I deeply believe that few people can resist the curative power of genuine care and help. Likewise few people can fail to generate a self-healing process when they become genuinely involved in healing others. This is the stuff and essence of cooperative exchange. It is the antithesis of competition: selflessness is the greatest weapon in integrating and aiding the self.

6.

ANGER

As I'VE STATED in *The Angry Book*, a book exclusively devoted to the subject of anger, this emotion confuses us more than any other. It is sinned against more than any other. It is perverted more than any other. More stress is created about it than about any other emotion, and that's why it is relevant, indeed extremely important, that we discuss its relationship to inner peace here in this work.

How Anger Works

Paradoxical as it may seem, recognizing and expressing anger are the best ways to reduce reactive anger or avoid getting angry in the first place. This is so because anger does not go away if it is repressed, unfelt, and unexpressed.

In our society the expression of anger is often confused with self-assertion and is therefore seen as a masculine trait. But at the same time it is seen as feminine if one "loses control" and expresses angry feelings. For many people anger is an emotion and a reaction fraught with danger. This is especially true of self-effacing, overly dependent people whose sense of well-being and safety is mainly predicated on being liked. In our society anger is often used to fuel self-assertion and as an excuse "to tell the truth," which would not be told if anger were not present.

Since much confusion and much anxiety and internal conflict are associated with this entirely human emotion, there is a great deal of repression of anger. But from birth on, we all have the physiological apparatus and the emotional potential to get angry, and all of us, all of us without exception, do get angry during our lives. When we get angry and repress the feeling so that we are not conscious of it—let alone able to express it—the anger does not simply dissolve. On the contrary, it sits there and festers. As it threatens to break through the repressive devices into our consciousness, it creates anxiety. Indeed, I believe that the repression of anger and its consequent threat to break through, and the individual's unsuccessful attempt to continue to repress (unconsciously) and to suppress (consciously), constitute the single largest factor in the creation of anxiety and stress in people.

Some of the anger is actually dissipated in the form of anxiety, and this to me represents one of the most important perversions of this human emotion. But much anger remains, accumulates, and eventually becomes explosive. Explosive anger is discharged in the form of acute anxiety attacks and inappropriate temper tantrums in which much more anger is discharged than the stimulating situation seems to call for. But much still remains and this too must seek outlet even as it evades recognition by its host. So we use other devices—perversions of anger—to hide or deny this dangerous emotion.

Peculiar thoughts, particularly horrifying and self-terrorizing thoughts and fantasies. Anger that is repressed snowballs and finally breaks through censorship in exaggerated, frightening form. For example, you may suddenly have a fantasy of a person (the object of your anger) falling in front of a train or being stabbed by yourself.

Anxiety attacks. These occur when anger threatens to break through to consciousness. They may consist of a combination of light-headedness, fainting, tachycardia, profuse sweating, disorientation, terror, a fear of loss of self, a fear of loss of impulse control (you fantasize jumping in front of a car), phobic reactions, panic reaction, gastrointestinal disturbances, insomnia, vomiting, forgetfulness, disorganized thinking, and more.

Self-hate. Self-hate in any of its multifaceted, highly diverse manifestations can be a form of perverted anger. These manifestations can be direct: self-diminution, guilt and self-recrimination, or second guessing; or indirect: illusions that detract from real self, exorbitant expectations or impossible standards, boredom. Just about any perverse form of anger ultimately works against the self and therefore must be defined as self-hate. Self-hate may be a form of direct anger at self or may represent a displacement of anger felt against someone else and internalized. Of course anger at self, expecially anger that is not conscious and recognized and that takes on any of the manifestations represented by this list, can be exceedingly damaging to self, to relationships, and eventually to others.

Depression. This is one of the most prevalent forms of anger directed at one's self. It is the most prevalent symptom of emotional disturbance in our society today. From my point of view, serious depression—the inability to get up in the morning, the tendency to burst into tears for no reason, the loss of appetite for food, sex, pleasure (all of which must be differentiated from appropriate sadness)—is always linked to difficulties with feelings of anger. Thus, the prevalence of depression in our culture is to me evidence of problems with anger in a great many people. Depression is an adult equivalent of a temper tantrum. It represents anger at one's self directly and anger at other people, displaced and directed at one's self. Depression dissipates anger, albeit poorly and at great expense to the self, producing much inner pain and malfunction. At the same time depression is an effort to put down and repress anger further. It also has a numbing, dulling, anesthetic effect that serves to deaden feelings of anger even more.

Suicide. Suicide is the personification of acting out rage at one's self and at others. It often occurs as the anesthetic effect of depression is lifted. This is so because rage at self may still not have dissipated as the individual emerges from deep depression. As emergence takes place the victim has enough newfound energy to act out self-hating rage at self as well as rage at others.

Psychosomatic disturbances. These are often the result of repressed anger and of attempts to discharge rage somehow, even through these perverted and destructive exits. They may include: headaches, muscular tension, destruction of gums and teeth through teeth grinding, disturbances of vision and hearing, skin eruptions, cardiovascular disorders (especially heart arrhythmias), fever and sweating, gastrointestinal disturbances including diarrhea, constipation, duodenal ulcer, ileitus, as well as added complications to preexisting somatic conditions unrelated to anger.

Accident proneness. This includes all kinds of accidents, and particularly automobile accidents. Cars are often used as weapons and instruments to discharge anger.

Addictions. Anger is often acted out as well as repressed through the use of drugs, tobacco, and food. Much obesity is the result of eating binges that are unconscious temper tantrums. Obesity has been a great interest of mine for years. The single most prevalent characteristic I find in grossly overweight people is difficulty with the expression of anger. Contrary to popular opinion very fat people are not at peace and complacent. They repress a lot of anger and suffer from much inner turmoil.

Explosive rage reactions. These are the result of chronic storing of anger, which eventually breaks through out of proportion to the igniting event.

Competitive sports. Sports are often used as outlets for anger, many times endangering self and others.

Vindictive triumphs. These range from sadistic remarks in social situations to "killing my competitors" in business.

Gossip. Anger is surreptitiously discharged by "innocent" verbal maiming and maligning of other people.

Sexual difficulties. These abound where anger is repressed. Unconscious attempts to thwart a partner's satisfaction as a means of expressing anger are common. These take place through all kinds of manifestations essentially designed to frustrate. They may include lack of interest, making one's self unattractive, "refusing" to become excited or to have satisfying reactions, impotence, or premature ejaculation.

It is almost never possible to repress one emotion without repressing others. It is impossible to experience prolonged relative peace of mind when a great deal of repression is taking place. Blocking anger invariably results in also blocking other emotions—of warmth, caring, and the desire for closeness—and this is not only disturbing to oneself but also to relationships with other people. Much blockage of anger is the result of the belief developed early in life that this is the way to get along well with people. Nothing could be farther from the truth! Chronic blocking of "warm anger"—and appropriate anger is warm and closely linked to other "warm" feelings, those of caring and love and tenderness and openness and intimacy—leads to the cold anger that destroys longstanding relationships. When anger is not expressed directly as anger, the problems, differences, irritations, or misunderstandings that gave birth to anger in the first place cannot be dealt with.

Making Anger Work for You

We human beings do not communicate automatically and telepathically, no matter how much we have in common and no matter how much we love each other. We *must* tell each other how we feel and we must struggle in order to communicate effectively—that is, to give straight messages. But we cannot do this if we do not know how we feel, if the messages to ourselves are not straight.

What this means is that, although anger goes away best if it is expressed at the time of its inception, it also goes away if it is *felt*, even if it is not expressed to others. *Consciously feeling anger is an expression of anger*, even if it is expressed only to self. How can we talk things over with ourselves and attempt to soothe ourselves and to make things easier next time if our whole direction is to prove that "nothing is wrong" in the first place? How often I have heard people with pride in "being nice" insist time and again that "nothing is wrong" until everything is wrong and a complete rupture of relationships has taken place!

It is of course very valuable when one gets angry to attempt to find the real source of the anger, for remediation and future prevention. Was it hurt pride?

Pride in what? Can that pride be dissipated or even abandoned (pride in always being right, for example)? Was it a thwarted claim? Was it a displacement from another source entirely, a source that needs investigation but is painful to confront (a man raging at his children instead of his boss)?

To the extent that we can *prevent* anger, and this in no way means *repress* anger, we are better off. But we can never prevent anger completely and we can't prevent it at all if we continue to repress it. Therefore our first priority is to feel it and to attempt to uncover it wherever it exists, that is, to try to prevent its repression. Expressing anger warmly, directly, and appropriately is of great value. In our society this is not always possible. It is possible between *real friends*. Most of our relationships do not consist of real friendships, unfortunately. But if we are to be at peace with ourselves we must work at knowing when and how we are angry. We honor ourselves and our friends when we can tell them how we feel.

As struggles for conveying true feelings, especially anger, take place between ourselves and others and, more important, between ourselves and ourselves, these communications become easier. Confusion and turmoil dissipate. Elaborate complications disappear. Relationships get easier and more satisfying as honest and good feelings emerge. Self-trust and trust of others increase. Subterfuge and rage at having to subvert self-truths, as well as subversion of anger itself, become minimal. Peace with yourself and others increases when you don't have to sabotage people to "get even." Hidden claims on others (what we secretly feel they owe us for our martyrdom in repressing anger and being so nice) become minimal. And hurt pride disappears.

7.

BEING OPEN TO GOODNESS

FAYE WAS A patient of mine, a terrible perfectionist for whom nothing and nobody was ever "good enough." As a result of her perfectionism she lived in an emotionally impoverished world. She had the illusion that money was all she required for happiness. One day she unexpectedly inherited a large sum of money from a relative she hardly knew. Her immediate excitement quickly turned to anxiety and pressure. What was she to do with the money? What would be the "perfect investment"? How much, if any, should she spend? And so on. Up to this point no attempt on my part had made any dent at all in her perfectionism and bleak outlook. Explorations of the past and investigations of the origins of her neurotic outlook did not change her. When further misery ensued following receipt of the money I pointed out her inability to be open to goodness and this she finally *understood*, on what we might call a gut level. From that point on, the work on her further opening to goodness and the struggle for change and growth began on a serious and productive level.

Let me immediately say that the goodness I speak of here has nothing whatsoever to do with dehumanized, self-idealized, otherworldly saintliness. Quite the contrary! It is a cornerstone of the mellow philosophy—and it has a direct application to improving life's experiences here and now.

What Is Goodness?

Though for the purpose of explanation I may speak of goodness and openness one at a time, the two cannot really be separated. Goodness itself, and the feelings, satisfactions, pleasures, change, and growth that are experienced as it is perceived, received, and incorporated in the self, *cannot happen* without openness. And being open to goodness cannot happen unless one is in the presence of goodness. Potentially, openness and goodness are always there, but they will not become activated in the service of one's self unless the linkage between them is made.

Simply put, this means that being tense, closed, fragmented, encapsulated, competitive, anesthetized, or alienated from one's feelings and emotions or in the process of deadening them—being any of these things —makes it impossible to perceive or receive goodness, let alone to benefit from its incorporation. (I use the term *incorporation* here as I would in analytic parlance—to describe the way we take in and make part of ourselves emotions and feelings of all kinds about all kinds of things, much as we take in food and retain certain nutrients, which become part of our physiological selves.) Yet when goodness happens, and we experience it and incorporate it, this incorporation of goodness sustains and extends our state of being open, and this process of extending and opening ourselves encourages receptivity to goodness. Therefore in thinking of this dynamism we must think in terms of the whole process of being open to goodness even as I describe goodness alone.

In the broadest terms goodness describes *being*. This means being on a *feeling level, a person here and now*—in touch through our own selves with the human condition as it exists in the time of our own lives. The first requisite of this kind of being is having alive contact with ourselves in all of our own humanity—feeling good about *who we are*, in all of our human manifestations. This includes feeling good in states of relative inner peace and during the processes of human struggle, which in large part are aspects of change and growth, as well as of integration and moving toward wholeness; it includes the physical satisfactions of movement, physical development, sensations of warmth, coolness, and any satisfying sensory perceptions. Goodness includes the satisfaction that comes from small things or large things—satisfaction directly proportionate to our ability to accept our own humanity and that of others without making cultural judgments, but always appreciating the struggle being human entails. This means looking back at the little children we were, and looking now at the grown-ups we are becoming, with empathy, satisfaction, and enjoyment, and in large part without cultural failure/success value judgments. Goodness comes in many forms and ways, and the separation between inner and outer awareness is only an attempt to pin down an ever-moving interwoven process.

Goodness is bodily processes going well—urinating with ease, eating with appetite, moving without difficulty, being able to take a brisk walk or an afternoon nap. Goodness is experiencing pleasant and satisfying happenings: a beautiful cloud formation; a ride in the country; the bustle of crowds in the city; a baby's ever-changing facial expressions; a warm, cozy room on a rainy day; a good book; snow; hot weather and an air-conditioned room; thirst and cold water; a warm bath; a full orange moon; a woman's smile; music; the pleasure of bread, butter, a cup of coffee in a warm kitchen on a cold day; a window-shopping tour; a movie; a play; an opera, concert, the ballet; the zoo; watching formations of birds; playing with sand; painting a wall or a piece of furniture or a whole house; singing; dancing; watching a woman put on make-up; the smell of good cooking on coming home after a hard day's work; being bone-tired; being half asleep; being fully awake—and of course the list could go on and on, depending on who is making it. Alive contact with such experiences is in itself an exercise of human goodness. But it also lays the groundwork for increased perception of goodness coming from outside ourselves. Empathy with others largely depends on resonant chords from outside ourselves making resonance with aspects of ourselves. This can happen only if we are attuned to these resonances. When people say, in the current vernacular, that the "vibes are right," I think that they are really saying that this kind of mutual resonance is taking place.

For there is goodness in sharing with other people the emotional or feeling space that constitutes the human condition. There is the strong goodness of experiencing someone's healthy change and growth; someone else's constructive struggles and myriad personal fruitions; someone else's pleasures, and anticipations of pleasure.

A friend of mine, a middle-aged man, conducts a monthly tour of museums, or goes to a concert or to a tennis match, with pre-teenage children. In so doing, he provides goodness for them and they provide goodness for him as he enjoys their enthusiastic response to these new experiences. Caring, involving, helping—being in the presence of the ongoing process of loving itself—can all be felt as goodness to those of us who are open to human goodness.

Of course there are other kinds of good things that can happen to us: the birth of a baby, the conceptualization of an idea or a theory, a victory over disease, and other "peak experiences." But their contribution to further reconciliation is small compared with the accumulated possibilities offered by everyday goodness. Also, it is important to differentiate between openness to goodness and seeking out victories or sensations with which to stimulate a deadened self. One is nutritive to the self while the other is designed to avoid confrontation with real self, real problems, and the real world.

"Laid back"—as the current vernacular describes the state of mind I'm advocating—does not mean laid up or held back. It does not suggest any kind of dampening of enthusiasm or emotions. It is synonymous with being openly relaxed, easy but involved. Receptivity and whole-person involvements are not possible when we are "uptight" and holding ourselves in and keeping ourselves back or down. But if we are open to ourselves and to the outside world, if we allow our feelings to flow freely, there will be very little in our lives that is taken for granted. Boredom cannot exist.

Then what blocks us?

Our society itself mocks everyday life; it propagandizes for power, riches, fame, "peak experiences"; it exalts the potential superlative and demeans the goodness of living as a human being in the here-and-now world. I am reminded of the question asked of children: "What do you want to be when you grow up?" The more interesting and important question would be: *What are you now?* In discarding the here and now we discard current goodness. This process guarantees dissatisfaction, as we trade openness-to-goodness for closure, enjoyment of the present for a fantasy of future glory—to the inevitable impoverishment of self. Although it is accepted as a truism, the notion that discontent leads to progress is a false notion; in fact, real human progress flourishes in an atmosphere of contentment or relative peace.

The extraordinary demands our culture makes on us for success, as well as the ever-increasing standards that must be met in order to qualify, inevitably *close* us to goodness in a self-defeating cycle. And disappointments with everyday life and the frustrations of thwarted expectations (money and fame do *not* prevent our children from getting sick, a promotion *doesn't* mean you will never feel under pressure at the office) guarantee cynicism and bitterness.

Competition is another powerful enemy of openness, even though, interestingly, many of us need identification with athletes in competitive events in order to initiate catharsis or some free flow of emotions. I believe that competitive athletics are largely residual, symbolic rituals having their roots in primitive, survival-instinct-dominated times. Unfortunately this kind of vicarious *treatment* is not lasting and not nourishing. I believe that where openness to goodness exists very little catharsis is necessary and little or no identification is desired with victors, victims, and antagonists.

Just as openness to goodness feeds and integrates the self, feeds optimism, feeds awareness and joy in being part of the human condition, closure feeds further closure and extends avoidance of goodness. I have a patient, Gene, who sat next to a woman he had never met before for three hours at a dinner party. They talked about all kinds of things and he could tell that she was as curious about him as he was about her. But they never asked each other about the kind of work each did for a living. They "skirted about it." For a while he felt like telling her even though she didn't ask "in so many words," but the information was never conveyed. He said that he felt peculiar after he left, "as if something was missing." He then brought to mind several instances throughout the course of his life when he felt "compelled" to withhold information about himself and inhibited about asking questions that would illicit information from other people about themselves.

Being closed to goodness can have a repelling effect. I have seen any number of young people over the years who suffered from intense loneliness and had no idea that their sullenness, bitterness, and cynicism "showed" despite very good looks or dress and even the "right" words. People could discern from the "vibes" they received that relationships with them would be antagonistic and full of difficulties such as envy, jealousy, or possessiveness and would be generally unrewarding and even depleting and destructive.

Being "closed" in this way can also prevent the occurrence of goodness even when it is thrust upon us again and again. Being out of rhythm with its happenings will cause us to repel goodness, even if we are the very persons who could use it the most.

Joe and Linda, two people I came to know professionally, were to have their twenty-fifth wedding anniversary in a few months. Catherine, a good friend of theirs and a woman I also know, wanted to give them a surprise anniversary party which would include about twenty mutual friends. The first thing that had to be arranged was when to have the party. It took no time at all for everybody involved to agree on a date, except for Joe and Linda. At first they could not be reached. When dates were suggested to them for social get-togethers—of course they were not told the purpose so as not to spoil the surprise—they could not make any of them. When dates were suggested much later than the anniversary date, they would not make a commitment because it was too far ahead and they didn't know what they might have to do at that time.

Joe, incidentally, had been complaining that he and Linda "didn't seem to be having much fun anymore" and Linda said often that she felt that their friends didn't really care about them—"I hate to say this, but I get the feeling we're being neglected."

Catherine did not give up. She risked spoiling the surprise element, hinting broadly that it was very important that a date be set up. This did not work. Catherine indicated that their presence was absolutely required. Joe and Linda still couldn't find time and offered the most inane excuses. Normally they are very bright, tuned-in people who catch on to most situations all too quickly. But their resistance went on. Catherine began to feel as if "I was being challenged." This may well have been true. Some closed people almost dare their friends to break through the closure barrier for them—a ploy that seldom works. In this case, after weeks of trying, Catherine became disgusted. She felt that the whole thing was largely spoiled and that the fun had gone out of it. She then decided to confront them directly. "The surprise be damned! Don't you want a goddamned anniversary party?" she asked them. "Oh, was that what it was all about?" Joe asked. "I thought something was going on," he added. "Well, do you or don't you want it?" Catherine asked. "Yes," Joe answered, "but too bad it couldn't be a surprise."

This was not an isolated incident. Joe and Linda had insulated themselves from good happenings for years. The claims they made on friends to break through the barrier were numerous and as powerful as the cynicism and suspiciousness they had developed over the years. Joe's everyday life had become a matter of suffering from one business victory to another, buying larger cars and more expensive wardrobes. Interestingly, he told me that when he was young and would go into a bar with friends, he'd buy a drink and leave a five- or ten-dollar bill on the bar, from which the bartender took payment. When he was done he'd leave a tip and pocket his change. But now, he said, he paid the bartender immediately and pocketed the change after each drink and left a tip just before he left the bar. "Guess I finally grew up," he said.

He gave another example of "growing up," attributing it to increased self-assertion. When he and Linda were first married and went to a restaurant with friends, the couples always divided the check regardless of who ate what or how much. In recent years, however, he had started insisting on separate checks. "I'm damned if I'm going to pay for someone who has more drinks and stuff than us," he told me, although he admitted that there was very little money difference in these methods of payment—the issue was largely one of "principle." But he also admitted that this issue of separate checks was always on his mind even before the meal began. Somehow, he said, dinners out with friends were not the fun they used to be. And his life with Linda wasn't as much fun, either. They fought more and more. Each felt that the other did not contribute enough to their marriage, and each felt "old," "dried out," and generally unhappy.

Joe and Linda still wanted goodness, and—even more—*needed* it, but through the years they had unwittingly become out of tune with its occurrence. There were many times when they had no idea that they were in its presence. Linda often said she could not understand why they had so few really good friends despite the fact that people offered friendship repeatedly; apparently she had a way of making hostile remarks to the very people she wanted as friends. Why? She and Joe also managed to alienate their eighteen-year-old son. Why? Both people were enormous strivers and in keeping with the culture were terribly concerned with "getting ahead." The were also worried about "staying ahead" and had through the years become increasingly suspicious of and threatened by overtures of goodness made by anybody who might after all turn out to be an adversary. Their world had become peopled largely by potential antagonists. They had become more interested in acquiring than in loving—acquiring things, status, prestige. Unable to love anyone else, they found it most difficult to believe that anyone else could love them. They wanted love. They needed it. But they had made a life experience of eluding openness to goodness.

Joe and Linda are not isolated cases. They are what we would call *detached* people: they see sustained relationships with other people as confining. A great many people suffer the way they do without awareness of why or how. And there are many of us who are much more closed than Joe or Linda. Some people are no longer open at all to their own urges to see other people and have shut themselves off both to inner yearnings and to outside possibilities.

There is no question that personal states of emotional health and sickness play an enormous role in how we perceive ourselves and the world. Detached people like Joe and Linda often deny the goodness that comes from close exchanges with other people. But it is nearly impossible to separate such personal neurosis from cultural disturbance. Each feeds the other and all of us are the potential victims of both.

Another woman I have been seeing for a while, Adele, was totally caught up in material acquisitions designed to "show off." She collected art work, bought a new wardrobe each season—not because she enjoyed these things but as a form of vindictive triumph she felt she scored over her "friends" each time she showed them something they did not have. Unfortunately her life was largely spent "showing off" and this left very little openness to anything really worthwhile. She eventually came to understand the sadistic maneuver involved in this showing off and the triumphal feeling she had when she stirred her friends to envy. Despite the momentary high she received when she was the first to collect a new artist or to wear the clothes of a new designer, she felt empty and depressed. She traced her behavior to fantasies of "I'll show them" when she was a little girl and felt lonely and abandoned by largely uncaring parents who were busy "scoring" in the world. I realized we were making progress when one day she told me that she was driving in her car and saw a rainbow. She said she felt strongly grateful for it and felt very happy that she could actually enjoy it. Several days later she said she bought a good pair of shoes and felt wonderful taking a brisk walk in them. "They felt so good." She said she had forgotten feelings like that. "It is like coming to life again."

Her openness to goodness continued to increase and as it did she lost interest in vindictive triumphs. Her relationships with people became more meaningful and "more peaceful" too.

There are many examples of the effects of openness to goodness. Let me cite just one more here. One of my patients, a physician, as he became more open, became aware of making increasingly accurate diagnoses and rendering more effective treatment with greater ease. This is not surprising. Openness to goodness produced greater access to much information he had stored, as well as sensitivity to information perceived about and received from patients. Perhaps more important than all else was his increased motivation and optimism about both treatment and results. This use of integrated self as an instrument for understanding and helping self and others is perhaps one of the most important factors in helping patients in psychotherapy. I've heard people say that some therapists have the "healing touch" while others do not. I think this so-called touch is largely a measure of openness to goodness, which in turn is a measure of the progress of the therapist's own self-growth. This "being tuned in to other people" is by no means confined to therapists and doctors. Many entertainers know this—even though they have not articulated it. They give to the audience and receive from the audience and as they receive they know what to give. What these entertainers get is much more than a narcissistic high. It is the enriching stuff of human substance; it is only possible where openness to goodness exists.

I believe that sexual relationships improve measurably as openness to goodness increases. Sexual feelings and relations are often extensions of how we feel generally and how we relate to others. But openness to goodness also puts us in touch with our own sensuous feelings and makes possible increased integration of these feelings with feelings of tenderness and the desire for emotional intimacy with the sex partner. It also puts us in touch with the other individual's needs, signals, and physical and emotional expression. In short, openness to goodness makes us *receptively* alive, alive in our giving, and tunes us in to ourselves and to our partners.

It integrates physical and emotional experiences of loving and thus leads to increased satisfaction in the sexual area.

Openness to goodness also improves our physical well-being. Our sphincters are relaxed. Our muscles have proper tone, rather than being stiff, which invites all kinds of injury. Our blood flow and breathing are easier. Our digestive apparatus works well. In short we are open to the goodness of our own physiological functions, including those autonomic ones over which we exercise no conscious control. Biofeedback and behavioral conditioning use this kind of approach in attempting to lower blood pressure or slow the heart, but sustained improvement in this area is more easily achieved in the philosophical and emotional state of being open to goodness. Individual exercises and applications on every level are important—as with competent sex therapy—but one's whole philosophy is crucial.

Are there people who are so rigid, so closed that they can never be open to goodness? Are there people who suffered so much emotional damage in their lives that severe pride, alienation from feelings, deadening of feelings, cynicism, paranoia, and impossible expectations hav permanently destroyed the possibility of recognizing goodness? I have seen people who have been in state mental hospitals for years get well and leave the hospital. I don't believe their improvement was miraculous. I do believe they were somehow put in touch with their own increased openness to goodness by someone else's help, someone else's real love, someone else's openness to goodness—whether that "someone else" was a therapist or a nurse or attendant or a friend.

Openness to goodness is not a substitute for psychoanalysis, nor does it supersede psychoanalysis. It *should* be a part of psychoanalytic treatment or any other relating process, professional or otherwise, that has therapeutic value. But being open to goodness may also take place without treatment of any kind. In Part II, I shall discuss a pragmatic approach to facilitating the process. Suffice it here to say that when we recognize that that process exists—that it can be augmented or impeded—we've already gone a long way in the direction of activating the process. In a way we are involved with a process which supersedes analytic work. The struggle to seek out goodness, to recognize it, and to allow it to enter involves a general attitude toward one's total life and existence as an alive and feeling human being.

Being open to goodness is not an idealized concept born of a saintly need to construct a utopian society. Being open to goodness is a practical way of life: we must be convinced of its value and must be ready to risk ourselves in seeking it. Some time ago I realized that everyone I knew kept secrets, especially about money. I made it a point to answer friends with utter openness if they even hinted curiosity about my financial life. I've subsequently found out that my divulging facts that our culture deems private did not in any way harm me. Actually it helped. My friends and I became generally more open with each other. We helped each other with money management ideas. And I felt relaxed—no longer a tight repository of secrets. I began to feel increased self-optimism as well as open optimism about people, the human condition, and the world.

Being open to goodness is vital to relative inner peace, because it promotes the nourishing relationships with self and others that make inner peace possible. When you are open to goodness, you are open to easy aliveness, to self-realization, and to the contentment, inner harmony, and equilibrium requisite for mental and physical health.

8.

TIME

TIME AND SELF cannot really be separated. Neither exists without the other. How we feel about time in terms of the rate at which it passes, how we see our own time relative to other times, how we use the time of our lives, and the value we put on time all determine how we feel about ourselves and the human condition generally. Our "time outlook" tells much about the quality and reality of our perception of being human.

It is important to use our time seriously—that is, to recognize it as a most valuable commodity. Since it defines the duration of our stay on earth, how could it be otherwise? But time used exclusively in pursuing success is not time used seriously, and much of what we consider "wasting time" is not wasteful at all.

Our lives are constantly changing. We are always in process, in a state of flux. Since everybody else and everything in the world keep changing, we can realistically say that all relationships—that is, anything and anybody relative to anything and anybody else—are really relationships between processes. So what is time, in this shifting universe? For me, human time or emotional time or feeling time or psychological time (any one of these will do) has two prime ingredients: 1) the rate at which we perceive change, and 2) the quality of change. Time is then a measure of that change.

A few years ago Jeff Rubin asked me, "If a person is constantly changing, what constitutes his or her identifying self?" This is an intriguing question. I think the answer comes from how we perceive rate of change and the quality of change—the psychological view of time. Let me first say that for many people the self-process is so slow and the quality of change so subtle as to escape ordinary perception. But time exists and no human being or any other entity successfully resists change, easily perceptible or otherwise. To answer Jeff's question, "What then is the self?": I feel the self can be defined only by a description of how fast the changes take place, and how they feel as they're taking place.

A proper description of a single self is complex (because it includes every detail of how that person negotiates the world in the time of his or her life) and necessarily incomplete (even as the self is described it changes). But theoretically, we describe what constitutes a self by describing the process of the changes it goes through. Each of us changes, or *lives*, in a particular way, and the description of how we change, including the rate of our changes, describes the self. Since I use the term *time* to encompass quality and rate of change, we can say that each person has a particular time, as he has a particular fingerprint, which gives him his individual self-identity. Obviously then, self, seen as a process of changes negotiating other selves and processes of changes, cannot be separated from time.

But what does this have to do with being mellow? Let me say first that I consider a culture or society constructive if it promotes individual proclivities in the use of time. A society that is appropriate in terms of the speed with which people can accomplish change is constructive. A society that is accepting of various differences in individual needs for different rates of speed is constructive. But a society that is ruthless in terms of individual needs and adaptation ability and that demands inhuman changes at inhuman speed is destructive.

Ours is a destructive society on all counts. The rate of cultural change is enormous and indeed has made the term "future shock" a byword. As stimulation addicts, we jump from point to point as the culture changes at fantastic speed and makes demands on us to change accordingly. But such demands for rapid change make all of life's involvements—especially interpersonal ones—superficial and shallow.

This *cultural time aberration*, which is inappropriate to human need, proclivity, and adaptation possibility, leads to a poor sense of self-identity and to great emotional vulnerability. The result is increased anxiety and stress—which in turn force us into all kinds of neurotic stratagems. When we believe that we have to be all things—for instance, when a woman feels she must be a perfect wife, hostess, mother, *and* careerist—we are brought up against the limitation of time. This results in still more anxiety and an emotional maze from which extrication is most difficult.

The pressure of time, whatever form it takes—internal or external deadlines of any kind—is an emotional enzyme or catalyst par excellence for the creation of anxiety. Anxiety is very often due to the emergence of repressed feelings (especially anger or internal conflict or hurt pride), but anxiety *really* takes hold in the presence of any kind of time pressure. Unfortunately, our society does more than demand greater and greater adaptive acceleration to change. It also provides what I call *time pollution*. We live in a world that is super-conscious of time. The din of time is always there in our mind and even when we think we have a little respite from it, it continues its clamor on an unconscious level. This starts out very early in life—even small children are inflicted with performance expectations in all areas by given ages. We expect children to talk when they are a certain age, to be toilet trained at another point, to have their first teeth at another; and when they do not follow this timetable, we feel they are somehow lacking. Odious comparisons are made and competitions are initiated as levels of accomplishment relative to age are declared acceptable or rejected.

Of course time pollution becomes compounded in the adult world, where "there is just never time enough for everything"—to attain in a single lifetime enough inflated dollars, inflated desires, inflated things of all kinds. Of course time is valuable, and time used in the service of constructive change and growth is particularly valuable. But time used to harass us further in quest of illusory rewards—time that destroys inner peace—is time gone malignant. *Malignant time* produces stress, anxiety, tightness, and closure and is antithetical to human health on all levels.

Malignant time nearly always seems too fast: it makes you feel that life has gone by like a shot. How often have you heard the question, "Where did it all go?" Sometimes having a good time makes time seem to go fast, but there is another "good time," a deeper, richer, longer-lasting mood of inner peace characterized by *slow* time—the feeling that time is languidly moving rather than harshly rushing by. (Of course, in serious emotional depression time sometimes seems to move at a snail's pace. This is largely due to extraordinarily painful consciousness of self and the desire for this burden of painful consciousness to pass quickly, for the time to pass and for the depression to pass, too. Relative to this desire for acceleration, time feels ever so slow and burdensome in states of serious depression.)

How we live our lives determines our feelings about time, and in turn our feelings about time largely determine how we live our lives. To refuse to feel that we don't have enough time, that is, to insist that we do have enough time even as we regard time as being most valuable, makes for a mellow existence. The interesting paradox is that we *waste time*—cheapen it by using it against the real needs of ourselves—when we feel we *don't have time enough*. And we use time most effectively when we *feel* we have plenty of it. Of course change takes place no matter what we do. Of course we get older no matter what we do. But we can have something to say about the changes marking our lives and the speed with which these changes occur. Moving slowly in relationships, in important decisions, in good work, and being still long enough to receive goodness are superb ways of giving ourselves time and removing the catalyst for anxiety and stress. (In Chapter 13 you'll learn more about how to stop worrying about time, and how to make it work for you.) Only *we* can give ourselves the time to be ourselves.

I shall have more to say about how the mind feels time in a book I've been writing over the years on speculations about how the mind works. But I do want to say here that in the mellow view, time is a continuum of life's experiences and changes as felt by the individual. This sense of continuum and relative smoothness is characteristic of inner peace. The current cultural influence on our sense of time is quite different. Time is felt as jagged fragments. People speak of different periods in their lives as if they themselves had had different identities in each period. It is as if our culture and its values undergo too much change to be felt as a whole with one's whole self and with one's whole life. So for many people life is experienced in units that are barely one day long. Some of us even feel the past accomplishments belong to such a different time and self that they cannot be used to offset feelings of failure in the present. Harvey, an advertising executive who told me he felt he was "slipping," refused to give himself credit for the string of successful campaigns he had been responsible for just in the last year. "It's as if another person did that in another life and in another time, like I've accomplished nothing at all lately," he said. "I guess it's the old story of 'What did you do for me lately?' "

A person's view of time tells a tale. This particular man is extremely self-judgmental, and his harsh judgments of the present are never diluted by past accomplishments. For him there is virtually no past, only brief segments of success with which he can compare current events so as to hate and torture himself into further accomplishment.

In the mellow time framework, on the other hand, one savors one's life, one's actions and inactions. Things are not done because they *have* to be done; they are done for the joy of doing them. This slows time. As time slows, more and more energy is diverted from self-impoverishing cultural demands and toward enrichment of self.

Unfortunately, time used for enrichment of self is often mislabeled time "wasted." A few days ago Alice, a patient of mine, said, "Yesterday I felt like having a really nice leisurely lunch so I took some time off. I felt so guilty. I wasted so much time. Afterward I walked around and looked at some store windows. Felt real good. But I felt guilty too and later on I felt pretty bad—I mean wasting all that time. But I told myself that it was a long time since I did anything like that and finally I stopped thinking about it until now."

Can having a nice lunch and a relaxing time be time wasted? This depends on your frame of reference. Obviously, in a cultural value system that demands "performance" and "accomplishment," Alice was "wasting" time. But in terms of care of herself and her needs, she wasn't. "Taking your time"—"taking it easy"—is using time most seriously.

This is especially true of leisure, an area of enormous difficulty for most of us. Leisure is difficult largely because of cultural time pollution and misconceptions. Life-long harassment of self in the service of speeding up time and using every second in slavish, compulsive accomplishment largely destroys the possibility of using time effectively for the self-enriching enjoyment of leisure. Indeed leisure time is often felt to be "time on our hands"—an enormous burden, a self-demeaning punishment, and a colossal bore. If it is "inflicted" upon us, as in retirement, many of us succumb to early death. We won't escape this "burden" by learning to have hobbies; we have to clarify what constitutes serious use of time, and use it accordingly.

I well remember the awe other medical students and I initially felt for the fast surgeon. It did not take too long for us to realize that the relaxed surgeon who took his time and operated with meticulous care was the man who was doing the most serious and fruitful work.

I believe that it is only during quiet times that real self-contemplation and development take place. Quiescent periods are necessary between periods of creative activity if things are to perk around in us, if germination is to take place. Thus, quiet or leisure or *easygoing time* is as much a part of the creative process and the process of growing and being ourselves as is the time of actual bringing forth or application or production. The former is the tree and the latter are the leaves. Without the tree there can be no leaves.

Sometimes we effect what I think of as a *time assault* with little or no awareness. My thought is of a man or woman who takes great delight and spends much time in preparing a wonderful meal, which is then gobbled up and finished in ten minutes or less. The satisfaction of preparation is not demeaned. The eaters demean themselves in depriving themselves of the self-enriching pleasure of a leisurely meal whose preparation enjoyed ample time. This is of course one of many possible examples of being poisoned by *time pollution*.

Is there an antidote? Once we have acknowledged the problem, we can establish a personal hierarchy of priorities—an ordering of what is and isn't important to us and a consequent determination of how and at what rate we spend our life's energy in accomplishing these aims. (I shall go into the practical aspects of this step in

Part II of this book.) This ordering of priorities removes time pressure because its premise is that everything *cannot* be done and *need* not be done, and that what we desire to do *can* be done with relative equanimity.

Time pollution is often ultimately traceable to fear of aging, to pride invested in remaining young, and to pride invested in staying alive forever. Of course the desire to live is healthy, but pride in immortality is sick pride: it creates a fear of death and an inability to cope with even the concept of mortality, its limitations and its finiteness. We cannot hold back time and remain young even as we speed up time in an effort to "live it all" and to "do it all." Even monuments turn to dust, as they should. To deny this is to deny reality. But our culture demands greater and greater acceleration even as it contributes to fear of that acceleration. The great antidote to fear, and perhaps the most difficult asset to attain, is humility—*not* humiliation, but real humility.

I speak here of humility characterized by a dignified acceptance of human assets and limitations. This includes acceptance of our finiteness, acceptance of struggle as part of life, acceptance of the fact that change takes time, acceptance of priorities appropriate to human limitations, acceptance of the aging process. Humility includes at least some feeling of being part of the human continuum, of what has preceded us and will be here after we are gone. It also includes a sense of how small we are in terms of the whole and yet how important we are as part of the infinite universe. It means that we do not demean the human condition or ourselves by attempting to be other than what we are or by identifying with a God-like ideal or attempting to locate God-like qualities in ourselves. It means using ourselves—using the time of our lives in a struggle for self-realization with neither fear nor guilt but with a sense of what is really is to be human and to have human dignity.

9.

MONEY, THINGS,
PEOPLE, SYMBOLS

DESPITE ALL OUR efforts to outwit time and mortality, we cannot transcend death. But we *can* live in a state of relative grace and equanimity, with full awareness of the inevitable. We can do this, however, only if we have an adequate sense of humility. The illusory conquest of time—our *cultural time aberration*—will not help us, and neither will worship of our culture's other god, money.

In its most basic and human context, money is used to exchange services, and these services are the stuff of the energy and the here and now of our lives. However, in keeping with the complications of a complex society, money has in almost all cases become more important as a symbol than as a means of exchanging services.

This kind of *symbol sickness* has infected many aspects of our lives: in some cases the symbol has become all-important and has been almost completely severed from the original source of its value. Expensive automobiles stand for wealth rather than a comfortable ride; the same is often true of the landscaping of private homes, art collections, associations with celebrities or important people, clothes, or certain "looks."

Symbol Sickness

We all know about "upward mobility" and "trading up" and the importance of ownership, especially ownership of the "right brands." We all know what gold, diamonds, pearls represent. We know that furs are for more than keeping warm. We know what "classy" or "having class" means and we know about the "right" schools and the "right side of the tracks."

We know that money buys not only things that we need but also things that will demonstrate that we have money. We also know that money buys prestige, power, respectability, and even "expertise." People who have a lot of money and celebrities of all kinds are held in special reverence, and advice is asked from them on subjects of which they may know nothing; notoriety is confused with knowledge, sophistication, and wisdom.

Unfortunately, money and its symbols have become the basis for self-acceptance, and considerable vulnerability to hurt pride and serious emotional depression has resulted. Over the years I have seen any number of men who had lost money—though they still had enough to sustain their standard of living—and were depressed enough to consider suicide. The loss of money did not in fact, in many cases, have any practical significance at all. But the symbolic significance of *losing a game* (which had become much too serious in terms of human priorities) was enough to jeopardize their well-being and even their very lives. I dare say that the many people who jumped out of windows during great financial panics still had more than enough money to sustain very luxurious life-styles. In our society, money and *the things*—we are a *thing*-oriented society—that represent money are delusionally seen as providing security, longevity, and even immortality.

The Wisdom of Insecurity

I love the title of Alan Watts's book *The Wisdom of Insecurity*. Money buys little or no security. The condition of being alive is characterized by insecurity. Some organization and planning may be constructive, but on the whole life must remain relatively haphazard. The belief that money has the power to provide secure, healthy, happy existence is a delusion. Money simply has no power against the insecurity characteristic of life. Yet of course our society preaches prudent investment and accumulation of money even as it tempts and goads us into all kinds of thousand-to-one risk-taking enterprises.

There is very little in our lives that is as constricting as the fear of losing money. This fear often makes for impulsive speculation resulting in financial disaster. Many of us see the money we accumulate as our very flesh and blood and as virtual extensions of ourselves. Indeed, this kind of feeling may be obsessional to the point where we sacrifice our lives in an effort to accumulate a sufficient estate to guarantee immortality. I currently have a patient, Robert, who spends much time with lawyers and accountants devising trusts and plans that will protect and govern the money he leaves for many years beyond his death. He is only forty years old and is in good health. But he isn't quite "alive" now—a great deal of his time is spent in pursuit of life after death through his estate. Robert feels that wealth lifts him above mere mortals and provides entry into a kind of earthly paradise reserved for the very rich, but of course no such place exists—the rich are as subject to sickness, communication breakdown, and other human exigencies as the poor. But Robert also believes that money left after death serves as a monument to the earner, who magically remains alive through the continuing power of his money.

In the truly reconciled life of inner peace, money has relatively little symbolic significance: it is only a means to purchase the necessities of life. Reconciled people do not have to create *synthetic aliveness* by producing envy in other people—they are already fully alive. In such families there is a relatively casual attitude about money—but the antithesis is true in "uptight" people and families. For them, money is an important power symbol, and an analysis of who is in financial charge and how money is managed tells a great deal about the family. Indeed, an examination of how the money is handled is often the best kind of family Rorschach. For example, in some families the man doles out allowances to everyone, including his wife. This often indicates, with considerable accuracy, a family in which the husband plays the role of father and the wife sustains the role of dependent daughter. Some families encourage boys to participate in money matters from a very early age but keep girls in ignorance. This is often evidence of proscribed and rigid rules regarding the roles of men and women in society, as well as of sexism and prejudice.

Many families use money as the battleground on which to fight out issues of all kinds, including intrafamily competition for love, prestige, and power.

Some families demonstrate compassion by using money to satisfy individual and family needs, while others use money to extend and promote a punishment/reward system.

There are families who demonstrate through money a fortress mentality: money, and its accumulation, are seen as the bulwark against the dangers, and possible incursions, of the surrounding world.

Some groups use money to express a sense of identification with superior beings, a kind of self-conferred nobility. In this group the ability to add to the family fortune is seen as a special family concern and guarantees a high place in the family power and prestige hierarchy.

Many psychoanalysts can quickly learn a great deal about relations in a family by asking questions regarding family money matters. This will reveal much that might otherwise be hidden for months and even years. Angers, resentments, envies, competitions, and other feelings all surface when money is discussed, because our use of money is often an extension and reflection of how we see ourselves. Some of us use money for pure self-aggrandizement, some for vindictiveness, some for friendship, some to be charitable.

Money is also commonly used for distance-making. Indeed it is almost axiomatic that friendship seldom, if ever, transcends money. We donate blood, make presents, or volunteer time freely, but aside from gifts of money for weddings or other special events, we seldom give money freely without the requirement of repayment.

This puts money into a very special and significant role as a definer of identity and self-worth. Both the potential "giver" and "taker" may see themselves as diluted or diminished if they give or take permanently without promise of repayment. This attitude is the antithesis of easy aliveness. I do not suggest that reconciliation requires giving away money, as Saint Francis did, to the point of impoverishment. I simply mean that an emotional investment in money that makes you feel you have lost a part of yourself if you give any of it away will make you "carefully uptight."

When we deal with real self, emotional investments of all kinds, the exchange of investments, the giving of self, do not feel impoverishing but on the contrary feel enriching. Openness does not entail sacrificial self-impoverishment. But it does make possible free give-and-take without the necessity for any kind of equal exchange. Where real self is in evidence there is neither fear nor danger of self-impoverishment. Compulsive or obsessive giving, done to allay guilt or to promote self-glorification through martyrdom, is impoverishing. But, *free-choice giving*, whatever form it takes, never diminishes the self.

Of course your bank account is not limitless, and I do not suggest that it be treated in such a way as to produce personal financial pressure. Quite the contrary! I am saying that devaluating money in emotional terms makes us feel easier and less slavelike about its accumulation and use. This if anything makes us more practical in using money, freer in using it—and more generous too. Being uptight and rigid and frightened and stingy does not increase prudence; on the contrary, it often leads to impulsive, destructive actions born of greed and confusing self-delusion—in particular the needs *to have* and *to do things*.

We have become a thing-oriented society rather than a people-oriented society. Things include every accouterment of "importance" and acceptability—designer scarves and club ties and expensive cars and the like. They also include the necessity for constant action, the dependency on always *doing something*, which we unfortunately inculcate in our children from a very early age. Society constantly whets the appetite for more *things* through increasingly effective propagandizing, using advertising and industrial psychological experts. The goals *to do* and *to get* give us something to "live" for—but we feel an almost immediate emptiness soon after *the thing* is either gotten or done. So we think of still more things to get and to do and these usually require money.

The climb involved in "upward mobility" is like the task of Sisyphus, never ending. It is also dangerous. As with all addictions, more and more is wanted and the task gets harder and harder, causing increasing frustration, an inner sense of worthlessness, a terror of poverty, agitation, and suffering. Unfortunately, the suffering involved in the climb, especially in an unrealistic quest for upward mobility, is often mistaken for constructive struggle. Nothing can be farther from the truth. Once the struggle for a decent standard of living is over and left behind, the continued climb is always in the service of stimulation and pseudo-aliveness through spurious self-glorification. This is not the stuff of self-realization. This is not constructive struggle and does not entail the use of money for healthy interchange with one's fellows.

To further complicate the issue, our society gives us an impossible double message. We are told that there is something crass and even dirty about money and that a preoccupation with it is somewhat sinful. We respond with secrecy about money and even with embarrassment. But we also come to believe that lack of money is embarrassing and disreputable, and that it makes us contemptible and untouchable. "Sharp businessmen," who take advantage of other people's naiveté and vulnerability, are condemned, but at the same time they are much admired and even idolized. And confusion, guilt, self-hate, and internal strife follow the impossible attempt to reconcile these opposing points of view.

At its most malignant, "money sickness" kills. Of course it isn't money that kills but rather people who kill for money. They kill themselves, they kill other people, they kill relationships. The ruthlessness that follows severe money obsessiveness is extremely destructive to one's self and often to other people too. A dehumanizing process that is the antithesis of being mellow often occurs. In this dehumanized state neither self nor other people are felt as being human at all. They are rather seen as kinds of properties, having value only in terms of money potential. This monomaniacal state of mind precludes human nourishment and produces a constricted, arid self, devoid of real joy.

Reestablishing an appropriate relationship with

money and becoming a people-oriented person again is not easy. Change always involves struggle, but of course healthy growth and struggle are synonymous. Motivation is of prime importance. Philanthropies in the last days of a life are of little consequence in terms of real self-enrichment. The earlier one establishes appropriate priorities, the more time of one's life there is for becoming people-oriented. Motivation largely depends on insight. In order to change, money-oriented persons must come to understand the poor emotional economy they have been involved with. In establishing a richer hierarchy of priorities, they must come to realize that life is much deeper and broader than money and that they have been short-changing themselves by neglecting the infinitely more important areas of living in which people always take precedence over things.

10.

AUTHENTICITY AND PRETENSE

MANY OF US cope with anxiety—whether it comes from money sickness, time pollution, or any other kind of conflict—by developing defenses or stratagems. Many of these stratagems are extensions of the images we have of ourselves, much removed from the actual truth of ourselves. We use pretense—what Karen Horney describes as the construction of an "idealized image"—to give ourselves synthetic self-esteem and false confidence. The price we pay is enormous in terms of increased rigidity, constriction, fear of being found out, and actual increase in anxiety. There is in this process a loss of spontaneity and a loss of use of self for self and aliveness. Much of this process goes on unconsciously and making it conscious is a large part of the work of what is now usually called ego or character analysis. Of course the degree of pretense is relative and varies from person to person.

Role-Playing

It is not possible to be mellow while sustaining a role. Playing a role precludes loose spontaneity. Pretending to be other than we really are consumes the self and causes self-conscious tightness. A chronic vigil is maintained in order to make sure we remain within the bounds of the prescribed role.

I was at some friends' house recently and watched their seven-year-old daughter "perform" for us for a solid four hours. This was not a formal performance and she is not a professional performer. Her "performance" was evident in her every action and her every word. It was all a calculated attempt to manipulate us into giving her total attention and admiration. I could detect nothing spontaneous in her behavior. The intervals when she wasn't being charming or interesting or clever were spent in observing our reactions to her in order to assess her success in getting the attention she so desperately needed. At age seven she is all pretense. There is no evidence of mellow real self. The child seemed tight and fearful that some evidence of who she really is would sneak out and be seen by herself and others. Of course, pretense begets more pretense and it becomes increasingly difficult to differentiate real feelings from pretended ones and real self from an acted-out facsimile of a superimposed self.

In many families, roles are unconsciously assigned to all members as they enter the world and the family. In some families children are forced into believing that they are "exactly like" a particular member of the family—parent, uncle, aunt—and are actively forced into emulating that person if they wish to be accepted. Kay may be assigned the role of the "good one"; Joey is "the bad one"; father is the authoritarian "strong one"; mother is the "compliant one"; Jane is the "prima donna actress"; Jill is the "artistic, creative, sensitive one." The sicker the family the less these roles

have to do with actual inherent characteristics or proclivities or natural desires, needs, or talents. They are
not assumed on the basis of individual need, but rather
because each family member must contribute to the
family's image of itself. The family constructs this image by a sort of tacit agreement: it is intended to be used
as a glue that will hold the family members together as a
spurious kind of team—"us" against "them." Of
course this promotes excessive pride, both for the family
collectively and for its members individually: each
member believes that he has a special position that
comes from belonging to a special family. In a larger
sense, it even leads to national or ethnic chauvinism.
And the sicker the family the more difficult it is for its
members to escape their assignments.

Some families—for whatever reasons—see themselves
in the role of intellectual bastions. Others see themselves
as crafty, shrewd, and as virtual fortresses operating in
a hard, uncaring world. Others endow themselves with a
mantle of nobility and feel that they are of a particularly
fine quality—the silk of the species. The assignment of
roles to various members largely serves the purpose of
attempting to resolve both inner conflict and familial interpersonal conflict as well. Each of us, of course, comprises many aspects. If these aspects of ourselves are irreconcilable we can attempt to cope with them by projecting specific aspects to specific members of the family. Thus Donald is aggressive for Pam who is passive
and Pam is lovable and compliant for Donald. Each
acts out the repressed aspects of the other; thus, by providing a cathartic experience of the repressed aspects,
each helps the other to continue the repression. The
price paid is continued fragmentation, unrealized self,
and dilution of aliveness.

In many people the strain of repressing aspects of
themselves and maintaining the "act" or "role" is enormous. Some of us do this during all of our waking hours
and then have terrible nightmares when we sleep and un-

wanted emotions are experienced in distorted form. Some people do it mainly at work, maintaining a Jekyll-like facade of equanimity eight hours a day and then turning into Mr. Hyde at home.

Some people have little or no conscious awareness of pretense. A friend of mine reacts to anxiety by developing very stiff haughty movements as well as a clipped, precise British accent, which is immediately dropped when her anxiety is dissipated.

But many people are chronically anxious and for many, elaborate roles have been assumed and have become permanent fixtures, replacing authentic feelings and self.

The strain is enormous and is often responsible for great fatigue, and a myriad of other psychosomatic complaints, as well as emotional depression. But again —the most deleterious effect is the destruction of authentic feelings.

Endgame—When the Play Is Over

For some people the elaboration of pretense has become so malignant that they only know how they are *supposed to feel, think, and act* relative to the created role. Sometimes, placed in a totally unexpected environmental situation where the role is completely inappropriate, they lose the ability to function (a loss that in its extreme form is the so-called nervous breakdown). Having no stage directions and no lines, they don't know what to feel, what to think, what to say, or what to do. They are virtually paralyzed, having exercised authentic self and real feelings and spontaneity so little over the years. This often happens when an unexpected change is imposed—a death in the family, divorce, loss of money, or a job—that radically disturbs the status quo, in effect destroying the play and the performances.

"Nervous breakdowns," however painful and sometimes dangerous, can signal the beginning of a struggle for authenticity. Although some people continue their lives in emotional disarray, and others rebuild the "broken down" neurotic defense patterns or adopt others, which again make them vulnerable to "breakdown," still other people sense that a large part of their difficulty stems from a chronic lack of the use of *authentic self* in living. These people are often motivated to get psychoanalytic help in order to find, develop, and use their authentic selves. The more authenticity and spontaneity we retain and the less we are addicted to pretense, the more adaptable we are, especially when subject to unexpected changes in our lives. In addition, we aren't afraid of "being ourselves," so the energy that was used in constantly being on stage can be recouped. I think of Sybil, who found herself exhausted nearly all the time, but who made no connection between her chronic lack of energy and her constant concern with how she appeared to other people. Sybil had come to New York from a small city in the Midwest and secretly thought of herself as an unsophisticated outsider, but in company she acted as she *wanted* to appear—knowledgeable, witty, always up on the latest plays, the best restaurants, the "in" place to have your hair done. In treatment, she began to realize that she was a worthwhile person whether or not she had read all the current best-sellers, and gradually she was able to give up the unceasing quest for admiration. Interestingly, the first sign of progress was that she didn't feel tired and washed-out all the time, instead she found herself "feeling more alive" and "for some reason finding time to do much more—what I like."

Authenticity and Relationships

Change in people who are no longer playing a role is easily noticed by people to whom they relate. Of course there are overt changes in behavior. Speech may change, as well as body movements. The individual feels and looks more relaxed, more comfortable, "easier to be with." But more than that, with an increase in authenticity people become more interesting. Pretense dulls people. Pretensions are repetitive. Acts are limited, lacking in depth, and constraining, and the repertory of pretensions is usually very small. Most of us are not "good actors" and we come off as cardboard figures, flat, dull, and boring. It is very difficult to have real communication with unreal people—quite simply, they are not interesting. But the return of spontaneity is immediately noticeable, and indeed, it is difficult to resist the aliveness and vitality of people who are authentic.

Pretenses are so common that we have seen them repeatedly in different people. Often, without knowing why, we feel depleted, fatigued, and dulled after spending time with uptight, pretentious people. This happens because their inevitable duplicity puts us on guard, so that we tend to fence with them and become closed and pretentious too.

Do you ever wonder why encounters with certain people leave us feeling "good," while communication with others is strenuous and depleting? It is the difference between relating and talking *honestly*, in order to convey real feelings and real meanings, and attempting to cover up, to manipulate, to compete, to be invidious, to impress, to be other than who we are.

For many people "friendships" are actually relationships constructed to act out pretenses. In many of these cases, these interfaces or interactions are an unconscious attempt to re-create early family plays and roles. These "friendships" are often frustrating and stormy because each player has his or her own needs and sometimes cannot respond to the pretension needs of the other player, often knowing nothing about them and failing to pick up subliminal cues. Thus, some of these plays become one-sided, lopsided, and short-lived. Many people cling to their families and return to largely destructive situations repeatedly, not because of devotion but rather because of their dependency on playing out and extending the original role created by the family. There are some families who have played out these pretenses so rigidly and slavishly that the roles and lines are never forgotten. Contact of family members with each other instantly cues the members to interact with utter fidelity to their familial roles. Some of these people can be authentic, at least partially, when away from home. But bystanders will sometimes be shocked by the change in behavior that takes place with each renewed family immersion. "It's as if a hidden director took over and made Mary behave in a way I never saw her do before." In a sense there is a "hidden director" behind nearly all pretenses, since the individual responds to unconscious direction and forces a good deal of the time, even when he or she is aware of being pretentious—and of course this awareness is often missing or turned off.

Some people are nearly always pretentious; authenticity in them is seen by others only when they are emotionally depressed. These "flashes of authenticity" come through because the individual's sick pride and the pretentiousness associated with it are temporarily down, permitting real self and authentic feelings, words, and actions to come through. Because depression sometimes paralyzes our ability to be proud and pretentious, it can produce a kind of pseudo-humility and an imitation of emotional health. Indeed there are people with whom we care to relate only when they are depressed. They make "foul weather friends" of us because it is only during times of depression that they are genuine. When they feel better there is a return of affection and arrogance.

Some people can be themselves only when they are humiliated, either by their own self-hate and depression or by others. Yes, some of us actually seek out humiliating experiences in order to be knocked off pedestals of proud, arrogant pretense so that authentic feelings can come to life, however short-lived. There are people who do this through unconscious maneuvers that guarantee failure. Others do it by engendering sadomasochistic relationships. Still others do it by actual self-vilification. There are people who are so frozen by pretense that they cannot feel anything sexually unless sexual encounters are preceded by self-humiliating acts.

Of course the healthier approach to reducing and eventually getting rid of pretense is the acquisition of real humility: acceptance of the human condition—including reconciliation to the limitations of time and other people. Humility is the antithesis of humiliation and involves a realistic and dignified perception of oneself, the human condition, and the real world. Humiliation and humility are sometimes confused because they may momentarily seem to have the same effect, that is, the restoration of real feelings. But humility dignifies the self and never involves self-injury or any "stimulating device" in order to attain the temporary feel of self. Humility is born of the struggle for reality and authenticity and the surrender of pretense, duplicity, ruthlessness, insincerity, and arrogance.

Our culture particularly fosters ruthlessness, or the "hooray for me, hell with you" affectation. This one is often used in the quest for personal "success," and I feel it is a pretense designed to deaden real feelings and real caring. Unfortunately it works well and destroys spontaneity and authentic relationships. I agree with Karen Horney that arrogance covers up fear and that the measure of arrogance is the measure of hidden fear.

I feel that this fear is largely based on the possibility of real self, with all of its human assets and human limitations, peeking through the shroud of affectation and pretense. Humility, on the other hand, represents both the struggle and the result of the struggle for authenticity. We develop humility as we become authentic and as we become authentic we develop humility. As authenticity returns a solid feel of self develops and this solid feel of self is humility. Humility destroys the need for and the vain hope of God-like self-glorification but sustains the on-earth rich feel of being human and having alive real feelings as well as the possibility of communicating authentically.

The struggle for authenticity is difficult. Indeed it cannot even begin until awareness of pretense and the destructive emotional economy of pretense is made conscious. Consciousness makes the surrender of illusion possible, but this is no easy matter. We do not readily give up illusions about ourselves and the world. Some of us are terrified that we will have nothing and be nobody without our pretenses. Because we have lived pretentiously for so long, we have come to believe that real feelings, thoughts, and spontaneity do not exist. This is not the case, and indeed our natural proclivity is not toward affectation but rather toward authenticity. We resist authenticity only because we have lived pretentiously so long and because we humans are so frightened of the unfamiliar.

Initial encounters with authenticity can be frightening and painful. Using a leg that has been in a cast for a long time is very painful. But it is very rewarding, too, when the cast is thrown away and one's leg is once again free and can be used freely. The use of real self is at first frightening and the risk seems very high. Some of us need help to do it. Sometimes mutual help of friends is enough. For some of us who have lost our way and whose resistance to change seems insurmountable, professional help may be needed. But it can be done and it must be done if we desire to live mellow, relaxed, healthy, alive lives rather than to play out wooden facsimilies of life.

Some changes in the direction of authenticity are quite concrete, even though they are also symbolic extensions of deep inner feelings.

I know a man, Philip, who always wore an elaborate hairpiece as part of a denial of aging and other human realities. His wig was a concrete expression of a good deal of pretense in his life, including the fact that he saw himself as a perennial bon vivant attractive to women half his age. His entire premise was a thin veneer and cover-up for deadened feelings, deep resignation, and hopelessness. I often thought that the wig was a feeble attempt to cover up all kinds of baldness.

After considerable struggle to find out who he was and what he really felt, and to regain sufficient life and appetite to know and to express what he really wanted, he got rid of the wig. Getting rid of it was not an act of willpower but rather an easy extension of newfound self-trust, self-esteem, and self-confidence. It signaled a change in other ways too. He became less concerned about other people's opinions of him and became interested in scholarly pursuits he hadn't thought of for years. He also began to enjoy relationships with people he had more in common with, and he gave up the role of munificent big daddy to young girls who could feed his narcissism with feigned admiration and attraction. They too had been playing a role. Even more important and perhaps lifesaving, he became less anxious, felt much easier, and "even relaxed," slept better, and experienced a marked decline in what used to be a fairly high blood pressure. When things became difficult, Philip was tempted to go back to his "toupee days" but he didn't do it. Authenticity was too interesting to surrender. But it is more than that. As I explained earlier, authenticity is, after all, the natural way of being. Pretense is the aberration, the reaction to anxiety, and the result of cultural imposition. Therefore when authenticity is experienced for a period of time, it comes with greater and greater ease, and as it is experienced it produces greater ease, completing what we might call a healthy or mellow cycle. Once felt, the sense of well-being that comes from being oneself and not straining to be pretentious is not readily surrendered for uptight existence.

Openness, a concomitant of authenticity, is also a natural human attribute, whereas being closed is an aspect of pretense and a reaction to fear and anxiety. The openness I speak of here accompanies authentic self and real feelings, as opposed to deadened feelings or feelings based on how we are supposed to feel. It includes openness to goodness, but it is something else, too. It is an openness that permits us to share real feelings, ideas, opinions, and thoughts with others. It is the antithesis of uptight secrecy. It is the relaxed expression of one's real feelings and thoughts without fear of any kind. This kind of openness makes creative self-expression much easier and is fruitful for everyone, especially for people involved in creative activity. Openness and authenticity and the real nonmanipulative charm and charisma that ensue also invite openness in other people. This makes constructive communication much easier. It minimizes the frustration stemming from the inhibition and breakdown of communication and fosters real mutual understanding and genuine exchanges. Here, too, energy is saved and life is made easier by relaxing the tension involved in holding back and being carefully selective about what can and can't be exchanged.

Does one know when authenticity has largely replaced pretense? Yes, one knows and others know too. The rise in self-esteem and the increase in feelings of substantiality are unmistakable. The same is true of the diminishment of vulnerability, hypersensitivity, and easy irritability. Frustration tolerance increases. Humor increases. "The edge is off most things now," as a more appropriate philosophical approach to life develops. There is a marked increase in vitality, energy, and the ability to have opinions and to know what one desires and prefers. And there is a greater ability to relax, to take it easy, and to feel good for longer periods of time.

11.

PAYING THE PRICE:
SURRENDER
OR CAPITULATION

IN THE PREVIOUS chapter I described how Philip, in becoming increasingly "authentic," paid the price of surrendering illusions. He went along with actual self and reality rather than fighting it. Fighting against self and reality—going "against the grain"—often produces chronic tension and pain; it should not be confused with healthy struggle, change, and growth. Fighting natural proclivities, sustaining illusions, ignoring human needs and limits, and at times even fighting neurotic drives (I shall say more about this a little later when I speak about the capitulation to "shoulds") all contribute to suffering and stunting.

A price must be paid for each and every move we make. There is no such thing as having it all. There is no "captain's paradise" where you, like the sea captain who has an unsuspecting wife in every port, can have the best of all worlds. Even the captain in the story pays a price—he does not enjoy the benefits of complete openness and candor with any wife since he can't tell her of the others, and he does not enjoy the experiences and rewarding closeness of an exclusive relationship.

Accepting the fact that *a price must be paid* makes an enormous contribution to mellow living and to inner peace. It makes reconciliation possible. It makes choice possible. Real choice is impossible and chaotic fragmentation is sustained whenever we try to avoid paying a price or attempt to have it all or to keep alive the delusion that we can have it all. It simply does not matter what the issue or event or situation is—a price must be paid. We can't do it all or have it all, though we often destroy ourselves to prove otherwise. No matter how efficient we are and how hard we try, we will have to give up many experiences in order to have others. There are many relationships and kinds of relationships we will have to sacrifice for others. There are places we will live and places we won't—we can't live in them all.

Surrender to Self

There are other "capitulations" we must make. As humans we will get older. Our bodies change and our needs change. We do get sick. Our children do have many problems. The unexpected and often the distasteful and unwanted will happen. Capitulation to the human condition with its myriad ramifications, confrontations, and realistic exigencies is a basic necessity for self-acceptance and makes life infinitely more fulfilling.

I am not advocating resignation, defeatism, or hopelessness. On the contrary! We must rid ourselves of the illusions, self-hate, and cynicism that ensue from futile expectations if we are to restore our vitality and hope to live well as real people in the real world. When we nourish illusions we doom ourselves to resignation, because the battering of innumerable defeats—which need never have taken place—forces us to surrender what *is* humanly possible. Sustaining some illusions can result in death, as in the case of my friend Charles, who—unable to accept the limitations of a damaged heart, blinded by an illusion of his own omnipotence—suffered unbearable stress and a serious heart attack.

We must surrender to the fact that we will *not* "get it all together," because there is no permanent resolution. But there is great benefit in the wholeness that comes of reconciliation. And reconciliation is only possible in an atmosphere of capitulation to (or reconciliation with) *reality*, the reality of humility, the reality of the human condition in all of its uncertainty. We human beings are mysterious and fascinating creatures—but we also are limited and vulnerable. This is the reality we must accept if we are to enjoy a relatively peaceful, happy, and fruitful life.

We must also surrender to our own individual needs, characteristics, and proclivities; otherwise we find ourselves in a state of chronic self-hate. We cannot ignore feelings without paying a large price. Surrender to "gut feelings" increases our capacity to feel and to recognize our feelings, and encourages that relaxed spontaneity which makes for inner peace and healthy functioning in all areas of living.

Most important in our capitulation to individual needs is the great force of special interests and creative talents. If we do not surrender to them—if we put them down and attempt to ignore them in favor of other, more "culturally acceptable" taskmasters—the results may be very harmful. Indeed we may have to pay a price we cannot afford. I agree with Karen Horney that creative people who refuse to succumb to strong creative urges become self-corrosive. They often suffer the consequences of alcoholism, drug addiction, severe depression, and somatic disturbances. The artist must paint;

the writer must write; the builder must build. Surrender to one's own basic needs and talents leads to being one's own person and an integrated whole person.

The same is true of our particular character structure or personality. We must surrender to who we actually are. Some of us are reserved. Others of us are gregarious. Some of us are inclined to be intellectual. Others of us have greater physical proclivities and needs for physical outlets. Some of us are restless and relax best in motion. Others of us enjoy lying around. And on and on it goes. Of course we can develop areas of ourselves that have been relatively quiescent and discover new ways and interests, but basic personality characteristics to a large extent determine the styles of living and relating that are most comfortable for us.

Psychoanalysis is sometimes necessary to reveal many aspects of ourselves that may be hidden under a heavy blanket of affectation and pretension. But it is not the work of good treatment to create a new person, let alone to make the patient over in the analyst's or anyone else's image. It is rather the work of psychoanalytic therapy to bring greater knowledge and acceptance of self to the patient, to make capitulation to the self possible. If the analyst has preconceived notions about style of life or the constitution of inner peace, this can preclude the possibility of constructive treatment.

I have a patient, Maureen, an artist who had been in treatment elsewhere. She was always in a hurry, expending a great deal of energy in frenetic rushing from studio to grocery store to appointments, and indulging in over-eating, over-talking. Her days were largely wasted in frantic activity. In part, an attempt had been made to reduce and if possible obliterate this woman's "turbulence." But, as a result of the attempt to reduce movement—physical, mental, and verbal—she became "blocked" in her artistic production and consequently became quite depressed. She also began to develop alarming stomach problems; she was afraid she might even have to have surgery. To compound her difficulties there were various outside pressures for her to lead "a more conventional life." In fact, however, in terms of her needs and natural inclinations, she was not "turbulent," although she was very active. Her life-style was not "conventional", but there was nothing destructive about it. When she surrendered to her natural inclinations, her organization of time and energy lost its frenetic quality, and she enjoyed considerable relief. Both her emotional and physical symptoms disappeared and she once again became artistically productive. Her creative work obviously flourished well only when she was being herself and was not engaged in the process of obliterating herself in surrender to outside taskmasters.

The "Should" System

Sometimes we suffer from an onslaught of very powerful inner taskmasters—*shoulds* and *should nots*: "I should be soft-spoken around the office," "I should have a spotless kitchen floor and all the laundry folded by four every afternoon," "I should not ever snap at my children," "I should clear off my desk by five," "I should never have to lose a day because I'm not feeling well," "I should always look my absolute best," "I should never let anyone take advantage of me"—the list goes on and on. (Try making your own!) We are never completely free of these taskmasters; they largely compose the rules we live by, which express the glorified images we have of ourselves. Going against these *shoulds* produces self-hate, which whips us back into line and toward self-glorification once again. There are times when we can struggle against some of these *shoulds* successfully and without great pain (for example, should always be right, should be nice, should always be in charge). But there are other times when we

cannot do this and when a futile struggle will result in
useless and corrosive self-hate. For example, Sheila has
a depleting and terrible relationship with her mother,
but she sometimes feels she "should" spend considerable time with her mother as part of her "good
daughter" image. From the real-self point of view she
does not want to do this. Her mother is not well and
complains about her ill health (implying that Sheila can
do something about it); she always says, "Why don't
you ever come to see me?" when Sheila visits. Sometimes Sheila can stay away from her mother and her
mother's onslaughts on her with minimal repercussions
of self-hate. But at other times her own attacks of self-
hate—in which she uses her mother's complaints about
her for weapons—are much worse than what her mother
inflicts. At such times I feel that it is better for Sheila to
capitulate to her *should*, her "good daughter" image—and go to visit her mother—in order for her to
be truly compassionate to herself. As time goes on, her
compulsion to visit her mother will be weakened, as will
the deleterious effect of her mother's attacks on her.
Until that time comes it is best that she take the route
that is immediately lifesaving—and I speak here of her
own, one-and-only life. This, again, is an example of
the inevitability of *paying a price*, and the wisdom of
evaluating the cost in a particular situation before
making a decision as to which way to move.

To achieve true inner peace in our age of anxiety we
must become increasingly aware of the flow and rhythm
of our lives—who we are, our evolution and development, the time it takes for us to do things, our assets,
limits, and tolerances. We must understand our
relationship to work, to play, to the people in our lives,
and to the world at large, in all its diversity.
Capitulating to our life's flow and rhythm, to our individual proclivities and needs is surely a large part of
wisdom and a major contribution to inner peace.

PART II

*PRACTICAL
CONSIDERATIONS AND
APPLICATIONS*

This section considers what we can do on a practical level to become increasingly reconciled, mellow, and peaceful.

Insights and practices are equally important; the following chapters discuss the use of both in direct application to our lives.

The chapters which follow are derived from the basic philosophy of reconciliation and aim to enhance philosophical understanding on a feeling level.

It must be remembered that there are no goals to reach; being reconciled or mellow is a process and, as with all states of being, it exists only on a relative basis.

I am certain that all of us can and will add insights and practices uniquely our own and of significant value in aiding the process.

12.

THE MYTH OF NORMALITY

IT IS OF prime importance to recognize that just about everything we've been taught to expect as "normal" in our lives is the stuff of fairy tales and unrealistic dreams. It is important because an enhanced appreciation of reality is vital if we are to attain relative inner peace.

The Smiths were a couple in their sixties who kept putting off having people to dinner—much as they claimed they craved company—saying they couldn't "really start living until the house is completely furnished." But when the house was finally furnished they found that some of the furniture they had bought earlier needed redoing and replacing, and so they put off "really living" once again. To put off living "until things are normal" will inevitably mean waiting fruitlessly for an entire lifetime.

The Illusory Norm

It is valuable to look back on one's own experiences and to look sideways at those of other people. This is not a simple exercise in being glad you don't have it as bad as someone else. Nor does it beg the question, "Am I supposed to feel better because he has it tough too?" or "What have I got to do with him?" No, the exercise is designed for further acquaintance with what the relative norm of being human is.

So look back and look around. Some people are beautiful. Others are plain but have a sense of humor. The most brilliant are often also the biggest fools. The shrewdest and craftiest are often outwitted and in some situations are downright dimwitted. The healthiest health addicts get sick and some people who are the most careless about health live the longest. Some mediocre plans and methods come out very poorly and some very chancy operations come out superbly well. Both the worst and the best die. Loved ones get sick and some get well. There are joys of all kinds—subtle and long-standing and sharp and short-lived ones. Dreams come true, and there are also periods of what seem like endless chains of crises, frustrations, and personal tragedies. One son will get into the school of his choice and the other "more deserving one" won't. The "dumb one" in the family will go on to live a happy life of considerable contribution to people, while her "brilliant" brother will become a chronically frustrated person.

People have problems whether they talk about them or not, and some will struggle through to reconciliation, while others become hopeless and resigned. Of course we can go on and on—the human condition is full of joy, sadness, limitations, uncertainty, insecurity, impenetrables, unpredictables, injustice, inconsistency, and enormous fascination and aliveness.

Does this mean that there is no rhyme or reason in life—that it is all hopeless chaos? Not at all! It is hopeless only if the illusion of perfect balance and consistent harmony leads to bitter and cynical disappointment and resignation. In fact the "normal" does not exist, and the sooner we realize that, the more we will participate in the real world, the insecure world—which is full of inconsistency but entirely human.

Patients who are depressed or very unhappy with the status quo often become irritated when asked to "look sideways" at other people in similar situations. They feel patronized by an attempt at an immediate but temporary shot in the arm. But looking around has a much more ambitious purpose than immediate relief. We don't live in isolation: it behooves us to know how the next person is doing—to feel better, not through competitive one-upmanship, but through kinship. And periodic observation of people's lives, including our own, can be useful for keeping in touch with what nonfantasy living is really all about. Reading honest biographies has value. It soon becomes apparent that celebrity status and "greatness" have little or nothing to do with inner peace or relative happiness and often even destroy them. Observing real lives and the real human condition is a good leveler and makes a strong contribution to humility.

I have a patient, Sam, whose seven-year-old daughter Ginnie was having difficulty with school friends—she wasn't being invited to birthday parties, and certain classmates made fun of her. One day he said to me, "I can't stand my daughter being in pain." I said, "Oh, yes, you can." At first he thought he had not heard me correctly. After I repeated what I had said he accused me of being insensitive. I said that I was being realistic about the real world and this included his daughter and particularly himself. Again I repeated that he could tolerate his daughter's pain, and in fact had tolerated many, many circumstances in the past—business reversals, the death of a parent—which he had at first thought intolerable. After we worked on this awhile he

realized several things. First, he had never really confronted the fact that tolerating his daughter's pain
might be possible. Second, there had been and would
always be situations in which his daughter and other
people would be in pain. Third, he could not remedy
every situation and remove every pain. Fourth, his
daughter was not at all fragile and had many joyful experiences as well as painful ones. She eventually made a
good adjustment to a new school; and I reminded him
that although she had reacted very strongly to her
grandfather's death, she had been able ultimately to *accept* it. Fifth, on occasion he could be instrumental in
diluting pain. This was sometimes constructive, but the
price he paid in anxiety and overprotection of his
daughter might be too high. Finally he came to realize
that rejection is a part of the *normal* human condition,
which is both painful and joyful—and only sometimes
susceptible to outside help.

The "Right" Solution

Many of us go on believing, despite repeated evidence to
the contrary, that all problems have a *right solution* and
that in all choices there is a *right* decision. "It's just a
question of figuring it out," we say. But most issues are
not all black or all white, and applying the words
"right" and "wrong" to them is utterly inappropriate.

In many areas of our lives and activities we cannot
and do not know what is the "right thing to do"—and
only by accepting this fact can we achieve inner peace.
Those who have a need for mastery and who have invested much pride in always being right suffer most
because of this, and lack of energy, destructive waste of
time, considerable self-hate, and often profound inhibition and even paralysis can result. The fact is that in
most cases there are many ways to do things and no

choice is altogether "right" or "wrong" but is rather a question of individual taste and priority.

Chronically seeking the "right" solution is often based on the notion that choosing "rightly" will make giving up other options easier and will guarantee no sense of loss or yearning for those that were discarded. But this is not true! However "right" a choice or action may be, we may still go on yearning for the ones left behind. But to the extent that we can pay the price, that we can discard options, that we can give up yearning, we can give up false notions of "right" choices and moves. In this way we can overcome the paralysis that overtakes us when we're afraid of doing the wrong thing, and move ahead smoothly—without painful head-banging ruminations.

Some problems can be resolved eventually, but the solution cannot be rushed or anticipated. There are situations that involve a number of people or other factors *you* cannot control, and these undertakings cannot come to fruition until their time has come—until all the other pieces fit into place. These are situations that require time for evolution and development—as is very often the case with creative enterprises, which may be spoiled by being rushed and pressured. It is important to school yourself so that you can discern situations capable of immediate constructive intervention and those whose time has not yet arrived.

13.

WAITING, PACING, AND RHYTHM

INCREASING OUR ABILITY to wait with equanimity is one of the best antidotes to stress. For most of us, having to wait is not easy and in many cases results in hurt pride and inner churning and even rage. This inability to wait and the reactive stress it causes occur in immediate situations: waiting for a bus, in traffic, for a movie, in a store; and in long-range situations: waiting for a vacation to start, for a school or training course to be over, for a "deal" to be consummated, for a baby to be born, for a stock to go up, for back interest to accumulate. Unfortunately, waiting is equated with and felt as time wasted, "a kind of living in suspended animation," "empty time"; as a loss of pride—"Big shots don't have to wait for anything"; as a blow to personal dignity—"Who does he think he is, keeping *me* waiting?" Although a great part of our lives is spent waiting for something or someone, comfortable and even fruitful waiting does not come easily.

Mellow waiting requires *awareness* of the problem, *motivation*, and *practice*. It is important to assess our capacity to wait without undue stress. This is best done by reviewing our reaction to situations that have required waiting. I know many people who stifle desire in order to *avoid waiting* for gratification, and then delude themselves into believing that this death of desire was proof of their ability to wait patiently. Of course this is not true. I know one man who barely allowed himself to be aware of his desire for a second home, in the country. He refused to accept the fact that he would have to wait until he had saved up enough money and until he found the house he was looking for. Instead he told himself that there was no point in embarking on the search for the house now—"One of these days," he said, "I want to find a place in the country, but that day hasn't arrived yet." He was pretending that he didn't really want the country house at all, and in a confused way equated self-deprivation with patience.

Do not try to avoid waiting situations, many of which are unavoidable in any case. But take advantage of these situations: waiting in business offices, dental and doctors' offices; waiting in traffic; for a lunch date; in line for a movie; for a waiter to serve food in a restaurant. Try waiting for an idea to develop and to evolve in creative work; waiting for a relationship to develop and become clarified before precipitous commitments are made; waiting in all kinds of situations relative to the business world; waiting for children to grow and to develop individual proclivities and talents; waiting for plants to grow, for a change of season, and a change of tide and temperature.

Learning How to Wait

After we admit and accept that difficulty with waiting is indeed a prime problem, we must be thoroughly convinced that learning to wait is indeed a great asset. Destructive commitments, abortive starts, poor judgments of various situations—especially of people and relationships—occur largely because you haven't waited long enough to analyze them. Without the benefit of adequate waiting, decisions are often made precipitously, without adequate information. This is especially true of destructive relationships in which "instant relating" born of great hunger for emotional involvement results in misplaced, overinvestment of emotion.

It is important to realize that most difficulty in waiting has little or nothing to do with real lack of time. If lack of time is a chronic problem for you, you probably do not know your own limits (or don't want to recognize them) and take too much upon yourself for a given period of time. But most of the stress involved in waiting is due to hurt pride: you have invested pride in *not waiting* and in having whatever you want *at once*. You think, "A big shot like me should not have to wait." Each time waiting takes place pride is hurt, you feel demeaned and humiliated and angry, and stress increases. Since professional training, serious education, the working out of business deals, or the evolution of personal relationships *all* require waiting, the inability to wait *must* produce chronic stress. In a complex society in which much waiting must take place, such hurt pride abounds and the cause of humility suffers; by the same token, an increased ability to wait with equanimity increases personal humility and its therapeutic effects in all areas of our lives.

Can we learn to wait peacefully? I think so. We must begin by viewing an opportunity to wait as a chance to rest, perhaps to reflect, and certainly not as an insult and torture specially designed for lesser members of the species. We must give up notions that waiting is a vacuum, a waste of time, an indignity that privileged people are spared.

Waiting must be viewed as a process that is a normal ingredient of all other processes. We must expect to wait, and must be prepared to welcome and to use waiting periods. I suppose this is a form of what psychiatry calls paradoxical intention, in which the individual is taught to plunge into the feared area and in so doing to overcome the fear. But even more, I also suggest that waiting be seen and used to reward oneself—a time of rest, respite, reflection, conversation. Some of the best conversations take place in movie lines. Some of the best perceptions of people's faces take place in doctors' offices. Creations of fine, soul-enriching quality take place while their creators are waiting for "more important" creative works to come to fruition.

We must give ourselves the *right to do nothing*. "Doing nothing" gives us the ability to wait peacefully; it is the antithesis of the chronic, self-destructive focus on accomplishment. "Doing nothing" is really doing a great deal for the self. It makes waiting possible; it provides the possibility of resting and the time necessary for self-replenishment; it teaches us that we are not mere work horses caught in the service of accomplishment and achievement. I must caution here that there is a vast difference between creative doing nothing, such as during waiting, and compulsive doing nothing born of inhibition, paralysis, fear, and anxiety. The latter leads to chronic erosion of self-esteem, and it cannot be turned off at will. Interestingly it often also represents a temper tantrum and an unconscious stand against the stresses and pressures of "always doing something."

Finding Your Own Rhythm

Pacing and *rhythm* are extremely important corollaries of waiting. I speak here of pacing and rhythms appropriate to various aspects of our lives, such as eating a meal or taking time for toilet functions. I knew a man who was severely constipated; it turned out that he paid no attention at all to sensations indicating that it was time to move his bowels. He knew nothing of his own bodily rhythms. Pacing appropriate emotional investment in relationships is of extreme importance. The pacing and rhythm involved in creative work are crucial. The effective writer knows he must not "write himself out" in one shot, that he must keep the associative train of thoughts and feelings going from day to day at a pace appropriate to the length of the work. The rhythms involved in athletic activities play a large role in the satisfaction you get, and the skill you exhibit, in doing them. (Interestingly, too, I believe that racetrack accidents in which horses break down are largely due to the trainer and jockey being out of sync with the horse's rhythm.)

Each of us has his or her particular rhythm and pacing appropriate to different activities—some of us require more sleep, others less, and so forth. But if we lack the ability to wait, we are unlikely to tune in to the appropriate rhythms and to pace ourselves constructively.

Try to evaluate your pacing of various activities: When you walk somewhere do you blindly rush to your destination oblivious to what goes on around you? Or do you look around, participate in street events, feel relatively leisurely about getting there, having given yourself ample time to do so? Do you rush through meals in four minutes even though the meal took four hours to prepare? Or do you leisurely enjoy it and possibly also the conviviality at the table? Many people, if asked at night what they ate during the day, have no idea; they take their meals and nearly everything else at a pace oblivious to human need.

Productive work—particularly artistic, creative work —is attenuated if individual rhythms and appropriate pacing are ignored. Of course the work itself suffers immeasurably if pressure is applied to meet business demands or profitable scheduling. But the worker suffers even more. If the creative process is not permitted to flower as it will, in its own rhythm, the artist may suffer emotional effects not unlike those that occur when physiological timing is ignored. Indeed the result may be destructive on both an emotional and physical level. The artist will feel out of sorts, fatigued, anxious; in some cases he or she may manifest psychosomatic complaints and may suffer heightened vulnerability to illness—and these self-corrosive effects may ultimately destroy creative productivity and lead to alcoholism, drug abuse, severe anxiety, and depression. If the artist, or for that matter any of us, responds to "a different drummer," that rhythm had best be listened to and respected.

Rhythms and Relationships

I believe that the area of human relationships is about the most important one in which rhythms play a crucial role. Instant relating *does* take place. There is a chemistry that exists between all people and it can either attract or repell. But serious relationships, in which more than casual emotional investments are made, invariably take time. They also take rhythm! They are a kind of emotional dance in which the participants must learn the steps appropriate to the kind of people they are.

A relationship does not happen on meeting, any more than a book exists when the idea for it is revealed. In both instances the spark is there but time and rhythm are necessary for the dance to evolve. Relating partners are involved in a process. I see this process as the evolution and development of a special dance or emotional language—a flow between the "dancers" of a unique nature. While this process requires at least a certain degree of openness and at least some common ground in terms of background, experience, and interests, it also requires time and rhythm. It takes time for us to know each other and it takes even more time for us to know ourselves relative to each other. Each of us is capable of investing emotions and of receiving emotional investment, of caring and being cared about, relative to his or her own unique frame of reference. The time that we need and the rhythms of relating we develop are, in my mind, the most crucial elements of compatibility in the progress of a relating process.

This rhythmic process of relating is not usually something we are conscious of and it cannot be contrived. But it is inextricably interwoven into the substance of our identities, defining the rate at which we become involved with other persons, the quality of those involvements, *and* the rate at which the other persons can become involved with us. In satisfying, constructive relationships both partners sense the rate and rhythms and quality of communicative exchange necessary for their particular dance and language of emotions. Insensitivity to the other person's rhythm usually goes hand in hand with rejecting the other person's individual needs and proclivities on all levels. Rhythms change as we change and grow, and therefore relationships between partners are in a constant state of flux. *Rhythmic* partners accommodate themselves to each other's new rhythms, without conscious awareness. Arrhythmic partners cannot do this. They become oblivious to each other's changes and go off in different directions as the music between them becomes discordant.

Most broken relationships are due to ignoring one's own and one's partner's rhythms. There is danger in instant infatuations. Waiting is often ignored. Self-idealizations are quickly projected onto unknown partners. Disparate sexual rhythms are misinterpreted or entirely ignored. Expectations are exorbitant and grievous disappointments ensue. These are largely due to initial overinvestment made much too quickly by people who have not learned to wait with relative equanimity and who continue to be oblivious to each other's rhythmic needs in the exchanges of deep feeling. Many unhappy relationships in which too much happens too fast can be traced to severe dependency, in which impossible claims are made by each partner on the other, all stemming from the basic dependency claim: You owe me constant, twenty-four-hour-a-day demonstrations that you "love" me above all else. When these claims are thwarted, as they inevitably must be, the disappointed partner's rage makes it impossible for him or her to hear appropriate rhythm or participate in the emotional dance effectively.

In that most intense relationship—that of the patient and therapist—trained therapists are well aware of the benefits of waiting and of appropriate rhythms. This is one of the reasons they ask the patient to wait until treatment has progressed for a while before making any life-changing decisions. They also know that until sufficient time has passed, interpretations by the therapist may be misunderstood by the patient and used destructively. Patient and therapist must *wait* until the therapeutic relationship is strong enough, until there is adequate caring about each other, before interpretations have a worthwhile effect. The therapist must also wait until he gets a feel of the patient's rhythms—how long it takes him to use and to digest different insights as he receives them—and must pace his remarks accordingly, relative to the patient's rhythmic needs, which change as the patient changes. These considerations are effective in nonprofessional relating, too. If there is mutual respect and sensitivity to each other's rhythmic needs, change and growth will be evident in both partners. Yes, the therapist grows too in a professional therapeutic relationship. If he or she doesn't, their therapy is highly suspect!

Learning to wait is not easy. Most of us are "late bloomers" and we must surrender our pride in being able to make instant adaptations, develop instant tastes, and acquire instant knowledge of facts and of each other—especially those of us who have a history of pushing, pulling, and attempting to tear out solutions and answers precipitously.

With waiting, issues often become clarified, problems sometimes resolve themselves, and we get to know what we really want. So many wants are impulsive and lead to bad decisions; inability or refusal to wait often contributes to the inability to differentiate between an impulse and a real desire. Compulsive, unrelenting drive destroys the ability to appreciate the rhythms of self and of others. It blocks the fruition of creative ideas and work and plows them all under with little or no satisfaction to self.

With insight and motivation, as a practical measure, I think it is valuable to make a list of areas that need slowing down and then to make an effort to do just that, gradually. Let me close this chapter by listing a few common examples. Of course each of us has particular areas that need work in waiting.

Walking: Walk instead of run. Smell the air. Look around. Watch people's faces.

Talking: Talk less and talk slower. Listen more. Give up getting in your own points for a while. At first this may seem like a terrible surrender. It often becomes an enormous relief.

Reading: Don't speed-read and don't skim. Read slowly. Give yourself time to have your own free associative ideas and memories as you read.

Eating: Eat slowly. Savor the food. Do have conversation at the table. Eating slowly is being respectful to one's own digestive needs and to the efforts of the cook.

Museums and galleries: Go through them slowly. Go back to a painting again and again. Try to get into the mood of it and to drift with the mood and with your own feelings. The paintings have a rhythm—the artist attempts to relate to the viewer's rhythm through his own, expressed by the artwork. It is best to see only a few paintings at a time. There are no points scored for going through a large museum in one visit. Learning to look at paintings and sculpture takes time and slowing down and relaxation. It takes considerable mind-emptying so that the mind can fill up with the painting and the personal moods and associations it brings up in us. Few other activities are as effective in aiding the development of languid aliveness as art and music.

Music: Music appreciation involves the most basic appreciation of rhythms. To the extent that we can give ourselves to the music and let it reach in and permeate us, we will receive the therapy of connecting with the artist's rhythms and will also develop our own. But this takes time. If you are a beginner at concert-going, give yourself the right to walk out on concerts, and seat yourself accordingly, until you get used to this very relaxed activity. As you become able to listen you will become aware that this process is a very active one indeed.

Sickness: We all get sick and it takes time to get well. Give yourself the necessary time, and live with the sickness instead of berating yourself, the world, and the human condition for letting you get sick. You'll get well faster and avoid complications and residuals.

Learning and training: These require proper pacing and rhythm—you must wait for your self to digest the educational changes you are experiencing and to evolve and grow accordingly. This is a highly individual matter. Many of us, in various fields of study, find ourselves saying, "I can't wait to be finished." Of course we can wait, and we do wait, but this kind of push to "be done with it" destroys equanimity and enjoyment and the educational process itself.

Losing and gaining weight or body-building or "getting into shape": Many injuries, some permanent damage and—on rare occasions—even death can be traced to "being out of rhythm" with bodily needs and physical tolerance levels. Health improvement programs require time—*wait* for your body to make its adjustments and adaptations.

Waiting for application results: These include applications for jobs and for admission to schools and other groups and organizations, waiting for acceptances or rejections of manuscripts, art works, architectural renderings, and so on. Our lives are full of these waits. If we allow ourselves to fall victim to stress and attenuation of function in other areas of our lives, we will inevitably be in constant disharmony with ourselves.

Life can go on—it must go on—while we *wait*; and if we learn how to do it, our lives can be much more fruitful and enjoyable. I think parents can be helpful in this vital area by educating their children from the earliest time on that many areas in life require waiting. Christmas cannot come tomorrow, on demand; and it takes *time* to collect enough stamps to fill a page in your album. I am not suggesting any kind of contrived frustration of the child. But I am suggesting that children can be taught that waiting is not an insult and is not a hurt to dignity. They can, over the years, come to learn that anything less than instant gratification does not mean *forever*. They must learn that waiting is not used to put them off indefinitely and that after an appropriate waiting period a promise of fulfillment is consistently honored. Of course no parent can make a child understand this if he himself cannot wait with equanimity. So to the extent that *we* learn to wait—especially for results of various applications, submissions, and endeavors—we may be helpful to our children also.

14.

THE ASSESSMENT
OF RELATIONSHIPS

JAMES AND STANLEY had been partners in a real estate business for many years, but their relationship had always been abrasive—which resulted in a great deal of anxiety and stress for James. James was essentially a self-assertive man with considerable creative ability, and he enjoyed putting together almost visionary real estate packages and developing land in new ways. Stanley, on the other hand, was a rather detached, resigned man: he was more interested in money than in houses or land or people, and he was in many ways the perfect account keeper. However, he always offered resistance to any new enterprise James proposed. The two men had met in school and started their business right after graduation, having known one another only slightly, and it had become increasingly clear that they weren't really compatible. Stanley, though, never thought of dissolving the partnership; he was too resigned to do anything that drastic. And he did not seem to suffer, as James did. James kept up the relationship largely because he thought it would be disloyal—and therefore evil—not to. In treatment James came to see that he had neglected to be loyal to *himself*, and that his so-called friendship with Stanley was destructive to both of them. Eventually they parted company equitably and without rancor: loyalty and disloyalty were never mentioned. Nor should they have been.

Most of us have come to feel, like James, that long-standing relationships must not only continue the rest of our lives but must also continue with little or no change. Unless we give up this belief there is no point in assessing relationships. The fact is that relationships do change, they can be changed, and they can also be constructively terminated, sometimes with the participants doing much better separately than together.

But assessing, changing, and—if necessary—terminating long-standing "friendships" is not easy. We would often rather suffer to sustain what is familiar, for the unfamiliar is frightening to most of us. And assessing relationships and making use of the consequences is frightening, because it means *self*-assessment and change in ourselves and our relationship with the world.

Most people refuse to see the unfamiliar as potentially liberating, interesting, and rich in constructive possibility. In the service of sustaining destructive stagnation, people will say they are "too old to change"; they are needed by the partners in question; that "there is nobody better out there"; that "people can't change anyway." All kinds of confused ideas about time, fidelity, and loyalty are usually added to relatively undisguised feelings of hopelessness. "But we've known each other for such a long time" is the oft-used phrase. Of course in this kind of refusal to extricate oneself from chronically corrosive relationships, loyalty to the self—the person one has known longest of all—is completely neglected.

Of course nearly all neurotic mutual dependency is fed and strengthened by time. In these cases fidelity to "good friendship" is a false idealization of mutual and destructive emotional dependency. Relationships involving forms of sadomasochism, from subtle to blatant, are among the most common of these obsessive mutual dependencies. These vary from subtle manipulation of each other to exploitation and cruelty. They are usually characterized by periodic reversals in role in which the sadist becomes the masochist and the masochist becomes the sadist.

Many mutually dependent relationships are designed to recapitulate early family constellations and relationships so that the various participants can continue to play out their roles in familiar scenarios going back to their earliest years. Sarah talks baby talk all the time, and defers to her husband in everything—making him the father figure and herself the baby daughter. Luke had a flourishing sibling rivalry as a child—he was very competitive with all his brothers and sisters—and now he has an extremely competitive and often antagonistic relationship with his wife. Margot's parents and siblings were helpless and limited people, and as a child Margot was always "the little manager," the responsible one. When she grew up and married she could not understand why her husband felt she was bossy and overassertive. These relationships are largely designed to maintain the status quo and their greatest success is in keeping the participants from the possibility of personal change and growth.

How to Know When a Change Is Necessary

In assessing relationships we will find some that are constructive and need little or no improvement. These are relationships in which we feel fairly comfortable; they involve people who generally do not leave us feeling demeaned, deadened, depressed, or having a sense that we have bastardized ourselves. These are "live and let live" friendships, in which the participants are permitted their own self-realization process without mutual expectations. This kind of cooperative relating *enhances* and *sustains* inner peace, and in fact may be seen as an extension of it.

Relationships involve mutual trust, and trust is a measure of our own self-esteem. Where self-esteem is very low, difficulties involving mutual trust usually ensue. When self-esteem is good and mutual trust and openness exist, relationships become vehicles for tenderness, intimacy, and human generosity and kindness.

When relationships have the potential for constructive change—when they can become *more* cooperative, *more* honest, *more* accepting of individual differences, *more* open to the expression of feeling—but somehow are not delivering on that potential, it's time to take steps to change them. Don and Frank, without being aware of it, have evolved a competitive relationship out of what could be a friendship: they're always *comparing* their incomes, their children's accomplishments, the improvements they have made on their houses. They have much in common, really, and they could in fact be cooperating partners in a constructive friendship. But they are in a race with one another from which neither can escape, and now their relationship has become constricted and boring. Don complains that all Frank can talk about is how much it cost to put the new siding on the back of the house, and Frank says that if Don asks him for advice about where Don's son should apply to college one more time, Frank will just "get up and leave the room." What can they do about it—and should they do anything?

There are no hard-and-fast formulas we can apply to determine which relationships are worthy of an attempt at change. But I think we can say that a relationship is worthy of the effort to change it if it does at least have some redeeming qualities. Has there been any evidence of mutual caring, of mutual help, of increase in authenticity on the part of the participants, of satisfaction in each other's healthy growth, of comfortable times together, of freedom to express and to share real feelings, of mutual respect, of mutual interests, of having fun together? If not—and if other destructive difficulties abound—this may signal the need to terminate the relationship. Have adequate attempts already been made to no avail, perhaps because one participant (or more—relationships may include several "friends") has little or no desire to change and even has a vested interest in sustaining the status quo? Very often the best approach to the problem is an open admission that both the problem and a desire to rectify it exist. If Don and Frank, for example, were to realize that their relationship was not satisfying them, and were to accept the responsibility for the problem individually—and if they were then to have an open talk about it—the relationship would have a chance at change.

In this case Don came to realize that he and Frank had evolved a malignant relationship, and so he was prepared to have an open conversation about it with Frank. Instead of a discussion that deteriorated into mutual accusations, they shared responsibility for the changes each sought. Their relationship lost its competitive quality, and each man grew individually. But if, when they sat down to talk to one another, the discussion had just led to further exacerbation, termination of the relationship might well have been in order.

It sometimes helps to involve a third person, someone who doesn't have any ax to grind in the relationship. The purpose is not to use him or her as an umpire or judge with whom to score points. The idea is for the third person to provide objectivity, to help analyze areas of difficulty, and to cast light on blind spots. This can help only if there is healthy motivation. Healthy motivation involves the desire to use communication, and people's services in aiding communication, for the purpose of healthy change. A healthier relationship is one through which each participant experiences growth. Unfortunately, some people, ostensibly seeking help, are really looking for ways to get further support for sustaining a sick relationship and personal stultification.

When to Break Off a Relationship

What are some of the destructive elements that signal the need to consider termination? The examples below may overlap; the big mother of them all is relationships that regularly increase affectation or pretense. These are relationships in which we find ourselves "not being ourselves." There are people who make us *self-effacing*—with whom we always bend over backward or virtually twist ourselves into pretzels in order to "get along." There are people with whom we consistently put down our own feelings, ideas, thoughts, and dissatisfactions for fear of hurting them, upsetting them, or incurring their wrath.

Some of us may well find ourselves having little or no difficulty with some people and great difficulty with others. You may argue—if you *do* have difficulty with particular types, such as particularly arrogant, vindictive people, emasculating people, or male chauvinists—"Doesn't it behoove me to develop strength to cope with them? Shouldn't I try to stand up to them?" But this depends on the value of the relationship and what an overall examination of it reveals. It also depends on your own problems and your ability and motivation to change. Of course you should try to conquer chronic self-effacement, but there is no reason at all to promote sick masochism by continuing to encounter sadistic, arrogant people with whom there is no overriding reason to relate.

There will always be some people with whom it will be impossible for you to have a constructive relationship without an inappropriate investment of time and energy. There are certain people who invariably demoralize us. If you've looked into your own part of the relationship and honestly feel you have acted candidly and caringly, *stop*. You don't need to strive to be Christ-like in an inhuman attempt "to get along with everyone." Termination of the relationship may well be in order.

There are people who invariably leave us depleted of

energy, vitality, feelings, and humor. Chances are excellent that we have been pretentious with them without awareness. There are people who are perpetual martyrs, or injustice collectors. There are people whose basis for involvement is essentially sadomasochistic: they have to feel pain, or inflict pain on others, they have to manipulate or be manipulated, in order to feel alive. Some people's feigned or real fragility makes us repress irritation and even rage, which they chronically engender in all of their "friends." There are people from whom we always come away feeling, I should have said this or that but somehow I never say it. There are people who deplete us and stultify us with their utter narcissism, talking about themselves and only about themselves year in and year out. There are people who will bring out lists of recriminations every time we are with them.

There are people with whom we never feel good. There are people with whom we cannot have give-and-take, forgive-and-forget relationships. See these people less often, and try not to take them so seriously, but with an appropriate "grain of salt." Treat them as acquaintances, not as intimate partners. This is sometimes necessary with certain relatives, with whom it may not be possible to break contact completely.

And if there is *no* saving grace for you in a relationship that you have tried to make work, seriously consider breaking it off entirely. This must be done in the spirit of loyalty to yourself and without guilt. As I've indicated in *Compassion and Self Hate*, most of us need much exercise in the area of loyalty to ourselves. Getting out of destructive entanglements is just such an exercise and serves us extremely well in the reduction of stress and in the promotion of self-reconciliation. In the same spirit it serves us well to seek out new relationships which make us feel good. This of course must be done slowly—you can't rush into a rich and full relationship, no matter how open you are to goodness. Relating takes time, especially if it involves mutual emotional investment and caring.

15.

TAKING IT EASY

IF OUR RELATIONSHIPS are destructive, the kind of easy aliveness that is the aim of this book is impossible. But the act of "taking it easy"—what I want us to do—involves more than relationships with other people. In practice, taking it easy—the easy aliveness that is the antithesis of stress—can involve relatively simple changes in the small details of life, or can necessitate profound, sweeping changes in life-styles and habits.

Where deep and great changes are necessary, especially if mechanical habits have dictated behavior for years, great struggle is often necessary for change to take place. Sometimes this can be done only with outside help, but knowing that things have been amiss with one's life can make the struggle easier, as can an appreciation of the emotional and physical damage to self inflicted by stress.

Taking it easy, with all of its implications, philosophical and practical, is especially helpful in reducing stress. Unfortunately, many of us are not ready to assess, let alone to do anything about, our feelings of stress until damage has already taken place, such as heart attack, ulcers, or severe chronic depression. In Part I, I described the origin and meaning of the phrase *take it easy* in my own thinking and the psychophilosophy it involved. I also touched on some of the broader aspects of its practical application; now, let us see if we can extend the principle of easy aliveness into application in your everyday life.

Periodic assessments of how we feel—about what we do, how we do it, with whom we do what, when we do what, where we are, where we are going, where we want to go and with whom—can be valuable, but only if they do not become obsessive self-hating injustice-collecting preoccupations. Assessments are valuable only in a nonjudgmental climate and are a first step in the direction of possible change. These assessments obviously concern our use of time, relationships (which I've just discussed), work, and leisure.

How Do You Feel?

In simplest terms these questions all come under the umbrella question, "How do I feel?" When confronted with this simple question, people who answer openly often reveal a great deal in a few words: "good," "bad," "hopeless," "meaningless," "drowning," "like a cog in a machine," "ground down," "pressured," "never lets up," "groovy," "trapped," "weighted down," "light," "nice and easy," "I'm knocking them dead," "there's no letup," "I'm having a ball," "I feel like I'm in a rat race."

If *your* answer to the question "How do you feel?" is essentially "Not good," then something is not right, and a look at some of the basic assumptions you make about your life may be in order. Some of the "truisms" of everyday life may need to be rethought, along these lines:

1) *"Getting even" is worthless and invariably destruc-*

tive to self. Unfortunately there are some of us whose lives are based on getting even, not only with our enemies, but also with our pasts—having had hardships, been poor, been rejected, having been poor students or poor athletes as children, losing games, anything. If this dynamic is present relative to any area, condition, or person, it must be eradicated or *taking it easy* will be impossible. The quest for vengeance puts our own drive and power *outside* our selves, giving the situation or person with which or whom we "must get even" power over us. We must restore central autonomy if we wish to take it easy and to escape from bondage to an Enemies List. Vindictive motivation is unrelenting in its demands. It is chronic and it tends to push other, more important areas of our lives to the side or virtually out of existence. Its obsessional nature makes us slavish participants in programs that wreck the possibility of inner peace.

None of us ever truly "get even." We cannot relive our lives, but we can go on with compassionate loyalty to our real selves. Loyalty to self, *real* loyalty, precludes slavish responses to hurt pride, as well as the need always to win and always to be right. Top priority in loyalty to self is to live long, and well, and *whole*, by satisfying various aspects of self rather than fixing obsessionally on only one—the rage engendered by hurt pride. The quest for vindictive triumph destroys satisfaction of other more important aspects of life, namely inner peace and self-nourishment.

2) *The show need* not *go on, and the mail need* not *go through.* The wish to get even has a destructive cousin, a confused yearning for bravery and fortitude. When we try to get even, our ruthlessness is directed against others, but in "bravery" and "fortitude" it is directed against ourselves. But as compassion for and real loyalty to ourselves increases, false courage (and its

cousin, vindictiveness) can be reduced. In our society, confused notions of courage and strength further cloud the picture. Strength is usually equated with rigidity and often with narrow vision, but *real* strength is derived from flexibility and the ability to change without fear of loss of self or of hurt pride and self-hate. Courage and bravery are too often forms of foolhardiness, but *appropriate* fear and self-protectiveness are evidence of maturity and the desire to live. Real courage involves the struggle to perceive and to encompass reality, to put down self-hate, to forgive and to forget, and to live cooperatively despite cultural pressures and influences to the contrary. Some of us suffer from subtler notions of bravery. The fact is that the show does *not* have to go on. We do not need a heart attack or acute appendicitis as justification for staying out of school or the office or away from social events; just being tired or overwrought or having a head cold is a sufficient reason. We must have the real courage to take care of ourselves and to be adequately tuned in to our own needs so that we know when we need care. False courage blocks us from knowing what we feel, let alone from exercising proper care of ourselves.

3) *Catering to pride is almost* always *destructive to self*. It does not build the self up.

Maintaining pride positions and pride deadlocks precludes taking it easy. There is enormous tension involved in chronic concern for "not losing face," in sustaining "a reputation," in keeping on top, in maintaining control and mastery, in making sure we get adequate respect, in being what a patient of mine describes as "the tittiest, the wittiest, and the prettiest."

The stress that pride causes has ancient and deep roots. Our early pride in being winners—in athletics, with members of the opposite sex, in school grades, in being in the best clubs—will later on be extended to pride in our position in the company, or the amount of money we've earned. Worse, these roots continue to put forth new shoots: I know adults who still take pride in, and others who still suffer because of, their grades in high schools Regents' Examinations, grades received thirty-five years earlier. There are any number of men who still feel inadequate and have low self-esteem because they were not good athletes in school. These men are not professional ball players; it doesn't matter whether they can field or throw. They have done relatively well in their chosen work as adults. But their old hurt pride still drives them. New pride positions may be taken in later life, but they are usually variations on old themes.

From a practical point of view, remediation does not involve concern over new positions as much as struggling to surrender old ones. If old positions are given up, new positions will also fall away, because in essence the roots of the illness are being weakened and even destroyed. If you wish to surrender your pride positions, I'd suggest you begin by listing them. Most of us are unaware of the pride positions we have, but nevertheless we suffer each time a pride is hurt. Tracing the pain to its source will reveal the position that must be surrendered. The "pain" usually combines anger, anxiety, and depression. For instance, if we get a cut in salary and suffer more pain than is appropriate to a loss of money, we may very well be dealing with pride, including pride in position (symbolized by money), pride in being special (let's say everyone else in the company took a cut), pride in earning more and more and *never* less, or pride in winning, which may be experienced as getting raises rather than cuts. Of course a cut in salary is not a joyous event, but some people suffer such events as profound indignities and become depressed for months. Identifying, and then giving up, these pride positions will help us take the first steps toward taking it easy. I asked Michael, a middle-aged, "successful" man I know, to make a list of *his* pride positions. Here is his list:

Pride in always being in charge.

Pride in never being helpless.

Pride in having a lot of money.

Pride in always getting the best of anyone in every deal.

Pride in being and looking generous.

Pride in "never being taken."

Pride in always getting a bargain no matter what the deal or item may be.

Pride in earning more and more money.

Pride in having the most beautiful and smartest children.

Pride in being noticed as soon as entering a room.

Pride in always being respected and admired.

Pride in being loved.

Pride in being smart.

Pride in looking and being judged as very manly.

Pride in always having perfect sexual ability.

Pride in always being a "nice guy."

Pride in being honest all the time.

The list goes on and obviously describes an idealized image of inhuman proportions, full of paradoxes and contradictions—an image that can never be realized. But it also describes vulnerable areas through which pride is hurt each time a fall from one of these positions takes place. The fact is that a person cannot be always masterful and at the same time always lovable. Nobody has perfect sexual ability at any time, let alone all of the time. Michael cannot get the best of every deal and at the same time hope to remain honest all of the time.

These "prides" guarantee constant attacks of self-hate as the real world is encountered by the real self. In order to circumvent these attacks, Michael has had to engage in all kinds of self-delusions and rationalizations in order to twist and to deny reality. Unfortunately, most people will not struggle to surrender pride positions until they have become victims of chronic disillusionment and depression often necessitating psychiatric treatment. But for those of us who wish to *take it easy*, this struggle is of paramount importance. Michael found out that he is a real person capable of much more easygoing happiness, without the need for being the best and having the most of everything.

One of the most destructive aspects of pride is the *pride deadlock*—any situation in which two or more people refuse to give up adversary pride positions, but indulge in enmity, bitterness, and sullenness, waiting for the other side to capitulate. This is how friendships end, family feuds start, gang grudges and wars have their beginnings. This is one of the most destructive factors in marriages and often results in their disintegration. Pride in locked positions invariably leads to self-corrosion in all parties, and nobody wins at all. Developing the habit of recognizing pride deadlocks and breaking them through personal capitulation can actually be life-enhancing. Suppose two men walking on a narrow street meet head-on and can't pass each other unless one gives way. If neither gives way there is a pride deadlock. If one gives way, he has catered to his real self and in so doing has weakened his pride; he is probably *less* fragile than the other man, who must protect his fragility by feeding his pride.

If we become aware that capitulation is inevitably ameliorating, we can develop the habit of breaking deadlocks each time they occur and of avoiding them by questioning their formation. But to do this we must differentiate between pride and dignity. We must come to realize that catering to pride destroys the self and demeans the relationship. Breaking pride and understanding everyone's position—that is, seeing a relationship as a cooperative dance rather than a cacophony of self-serving antagonists—dignifies the relationship and enriches the self.

4) *Surrendering the* now *for pie in the sky guarantees destruction of self.* This does not mean that we surrender our ability to conceptualize the future. It does mean that we do not demean our current experiences by constantly thinking of *tomorrow* as the "real time of our lives." Many of us are chronically dissatisfied with our lives, as part of our self-flagellation in quest of greater and greater glory; but when we demean the *now* in favor of the future, we are actually condemning our present actions and relationships, in a form of self-contempt that keeps us running after nonexistent goals—the antithesis of *taking it easy*. The antidote is to dignify our *now* by appreciation of all the good and human things that go on in it. Each *now* represents the only time of our lives.

5) *Inertia can be destructive and stressful if your current situation is antithetical to your real tastes, interests, and desires.* This simply means that you cannot *take it easy*, however much the world admires your position and accomplishments, if your own individual needs and yearnings are not fulfilled. We must listen to and respect each of our different drummers—even if their beat is not culturally approved—or risk disturbing our inner peace over long periods of time. We cannot always avoid change; for inner peace to be possible, we must be who we are, even if it means surrendering positions that other people say *they* would be grateful for.

6) *Seeing the world, its people, and ourselves in narrow right-and-wrong terms promotes self-hate, hostility toward others, and stress, cynicism, and bitterness.* My

patient Geraldine thought her husband was shallow and irresponsible because he loved hiking, bird-watching, playing golf, or just having a few friends over for dinner. This behavior, she thought, was "wrong." The fact is that Harry, her husband, was responsible, involved, mature, and caring. Her own restlessness—which prompted her to seek stimulation and competition in what she called, only half-deprecatingly, "my pressure-cooker job"—became more exaggerated in contrast to Harry's placidity. In truth she secretly envied him; but eventually she came to understand this, and she began to enjoy just relaxing at home with him as she became more reconciled to her own "tributary selves."

To the extent that we respect our own individual proclivities, we have increased ability to respect other people's. *Inner chaos* and rejection of self, like Geraldine's, produce envy, paranoia, and intolerance of other people who seek their own individual satisfactions, but *inner peace* seeks out and aids peace in others.

The best cooperative relationships are not those in which we attempt to win each other over to our own ways of seeing things and to our own satisfactions; they are the relationships in which we try to understand and to respect the other person's *self*. We help our cause still more when we aid in the other person's individual development, encouraging him or her to find and satisfy his or her own inner needs, especially those that are different from our own. (Geraldine, for instance, eventually grew to enjoy weekend golf games with Harry, even when she didn't win.) This is the antithesis of proselytizing our own positions. This applies to all relationships, but is particularly important and constructive between parent and child.

7) *The refusal to take a loss and to move on is the arch-enemy of taking it easy and of inner comfort.* If you

must always "recoup," you will destroy your perception and end up spending time and energy on self-hate, stress, and paralysis. We cannot "win them all," indeed, there are many instances in which we cannot even be smart. Pride in always being "right" leads to rationalization, distortion, and fear of participation and is the enemy par excellence of *taking it easy*.

"The Readiness Is All"

Of course *taking it easy* involves just about all aspects of the philosophy of this book. Therefore, any practical measures taken against stress are constructive. In this chapter I have attempted to suggest some, and each of us will have others to add. This chapter can be seen as a kind of starter course of action, and in closing let me make a few more suggestions.

Chronic anticipation in an attempt to control all of life's possible confrontations makes it impossible to be peaceful or easygoing. I am not against sensible planning, but such anticipation is too often designed to keep life smooth by the avoidance of *every* kind of conceivable pitfall. It is also an attempt to stop time, to bring the future into the present, and to prevent the evolution of life and events. This destroys the possibility of enjoying each here-and-now as it arrives, making for an uptight, arid, and constricted existence. For people who are chronic security seekers through anticipation, who spend their lives buying this stock before it goes up, or selling gold before it goes down, it is valuable to review past anticipations and to appreciate the enormous waste of time and energy they have caused.

Make a concerted effort to drop anticipation and to confront each issue as it comes up. Allow events in your life to evolve easily, without chronic attempts to force conclusions prematurely. It is possible eventually to have confidence in oneself and one's ability to confront oncoming events in life without the chronic worry characteristic of inappropriate anticipation.

Initial anxiety generated by this change eventually gives way to much easier living. In this connection, I often hear myself say, "Let it be" or "We will see." I think what I mean by the first is, let *now* be *now*, and don't spoil it with what *will* arrive, let alone with what will never arrive. The second statement means let us look at what arises if and when it does and not until then. There is a wonderful moment at the end of Shakespeare's *Hamlet* in which we realize that Hamlet is about to go into a duel knowing—or at least suspecting—that there will be foul play and he will be killed. His friend Horatio pleads with him not to place himself in possible danger, but Hamlet says to him, "There is special providence in the fall of a sparrow. If it be now, 'tis not to come; if it be not to come, it will be now; if it be not now, yet it will come: the readiness is all. Since no man has aught of what he leaves, what is't to leave betimes?" This from the man who, when the play began, felt that he and he alone was responsible for—and could change—the whole state of his world.

A final word for this chapter. I think it is imperative that we stand up to *insatiability* whenever we recognize it. This may come from relatives, particularly parents, who feel we've not accomplished or done enough, and especially from ourselves. Of course insatiability—wanting more of everything: money, fame, power, collector's items, stronger and stronger sensations—is a killer of inner peace. Of course there are things we may not have enough of, but our culture generally leads us to a malignant and chronic quest for more of everything beyond reasonable needs and desires.

Many of us, without awareness, engage in a form of "overkill": we never have enough money, lose enough weight, work hard enough, have enough conquests (a pathological outlook to begin with), have enough fame, have enough power. There are so many people who overshoot the goals they originally had in mind and become caught in meaningless momentum that takes them away from self and often away from life too.

I had one man in treatment who chronically felt "empty and purposeless." His name is Jack and he is a businessman who came from a very poor and generally deprived background. His original purpose was to make enough money so that he could pursue creative activity, both writing and painting. When he came to see me it was largely because he felt "empty" and felt that his life had no "real meaning." He had no ability to "relax" or to enjoy leisure time; he said, "I've lost the feel of myself." Jack had been a multimillionaire for at least ten years before coming to see me but he continued to work as hard as he had when he started. He had almost completely forgotten about his early artistic aspirations and goals, and indeed we came across them almost by accident. In talking about a painting his wife bought he mentioned parenthetically that he once liked "to shmear and to scribble." Though he resisted, I insisted that we go back in time and fully explore his past involvement in painting and writing. To his surprise it turned out that these were strong desires and occupied much of his time and energy as a youngster and that at one time he also did very good work. He was even more surprised at the extent to which this whole aspect of his life had been blotted out and abandoned. He felt that his artistic talents had been "crushed, ground up, and lost in the rat race of many years." The fact is that Jack was afraid to get out of the rat race. He had been in it so long and was so caught in the momentum and so distant from the most vital aspect of himself that he equated self with making money. He saw giving up the quest for still more money as giving up what little self and sense of identity he had. Of course his environment, among other businessmen in the business world, did not encourage further exploration. But Jack was lucky: he realized that making more millions "does not serve any real purpose but is just a thing to do." And unlike many less fortunate men, he was well in touch with his sense of emptiness and showed great willingness to struggle for easy aliveness. This made it possible for him to get out of the grinding rat race, to explore real values and desires, and to revitalize important aspects of self, his creative aspirations and satisfactions.

Jack has recently begun to paint again and this has made him feel better than any business deal he's made in years.

16.

DEADLINES, RESOLUTIONS, OBLIGATIONS

MY PATIENT THE artist had spent almost a lifetime meeting cultural deadlines—not his own. Fortunately, he extricated himself, but without struggle this is not always possible. Contracts with self of any kind have the potential to create stress far beyond those made with other people. Contracts with self are often thinly disguised collaborations with society's *shoulds* and are designed to build pride positions and self-idealizations. These may come in the form of deadlines, resolutions, or a sense of obligation, but they are almost always forces that work in the service of internal tyranny. They are nearly always connected to willpower or discipline rather than to insight or evolution. When we do something because of personal insight and real desire rather than out of a wish for self-glorification or self-martyrdom (one is as competitive as the other), willpower seldom plays a significant role. These activities are not pushed upon us by ourselves out of a sense of obligation. Indeed, they occur as an integral part of development and evolve with appropriate timing and pacing. In the case of self-imposed deadlines, self-hate often follows any breach of resolution. In the case of free action born of free choice, less-than-perfect performance and, in the case of delays in action, compassion for self are always present.

Contracts with Illusion

A self-imposed contract of any variety is almost always used as a prod to overcome inertia. But the price paid for the use of this kind of "motivation" is too high. I've worked with people who want to lose weight and keep it off, and the plain fact is that until *they* believe they should lose weight (as opposed to society telling them they should), they won't lose weight, or if they do, they'll gain it back. Successful weight loss never comes from "willpower" or reward/punishment blackmail devices. A painter cannot paint a masterpiece just because financial need or his desire for acceptance tells him to. What is there is there, when it is there, and we must not force the issue. To make a resolution or set a deadline is to apply a blanket solution to a problem that may have complicated ramifications. This is oversimplistic and self-hating, and robs us of the dignity we all deserve.

People who beset themselves with resolutions and deadlines often seem to be particularly humble. This is seldom the case. What appears to be humility usually turns out to be pseudohumility. The obsessive process of becoming a "better" person through resolutions of all kinds is rooted in unconscious self-aggrandizing. The resolver usually believes that his or her becoming better or thinner or whatever affects other people much more than it actually does. The principal unconscious factor is often the hidden desire to affect other people and in some cases even to be in charge of their lives, through "goodness," of course. The danger here is seldom to other people. The real danger is stress on the individual, who suffers chronic pressure from being ill-prepared to cope with inappropriate commands from self-hating aspects of self.

One's idealized image desires pride satisfactions without regard for real capacity, real ability, real appropriateness, or realistic timing. The real self seldom if ever uses the goads of resolutions, deadlines, or illusory obligations, or those other goads used to whip the self when resolutions are broken or deadlines passed. These include the full range of self-hate mechanisms: guilt, recriminations, depression, anxiety. Whatever is done as a function of real self is done because its time has arrived; it is part of a natural and unpressured evolvement. This is similar to the normal and natural birth of a baby whose time for delivery has arrived without superimposed deadlines of any kind.

Pressured Priorities

Many people are extremely sensitive to any kind of coercion or even imagined coercion. But there are also people who live in a constant state of coercion, to which they respond slavishly. These people produce obligations where they don't exist. They take on responsibilities inappropriately. They construct mythical deadlines that keep them in a state of turmoil and stress. Many suffer from chronic guilt and uneasiness, feeling always that some job is left undone, some deadline is not being met, even though none can be found because none realistically exists.

These overscrupulous victims represent exaggerations of what goes on in so many of us who habitually impose schedules on ourselves as a means of stimulation and "in order to get things done." Many of us also chronically suffer from tension without being aware that it comes from a general feeling of "not being caught up," of "everyone else will get ahead," of "I will be left behind"—whether the person we can't catch up with is someone else, or our own selves. Of course this is intimately linked to the competitive, success syndrome and is highly destructive of inner peace. In many cases a vicious circle is constructed in which we coerce ourselves with resolution and then respond to the coercion rebelliously, not fulfilling the contract. This leads to self-hate, further resolution, and further reactive rebellion, which may eventually lead to hopelessness, resignation, and in some people to paralyzing nonfunction.

Contracts that impose deadlines like these are nearly always oblivious to real needs, real conditions of readiness and development, or real mood and feeling. I speak here of being in the mood or proper frame of mind to do a particular thing or job. People may argue that if they wait they will never be in the mood and will never do anything. This is almost never true. When it is at all true it is due to the fact that the individual has lost touch with feelings and moods and does not take them seriously. When this condition exists it does so because one's own moods, feelings, and pacing have been ignored and replaced by dehumanizing schedules, resolutions, and contracts.

Be wary of contracts, especially ones you impose yourself. Be careful of those imposed by others too. Resist the bastardization of time—that is, the *use* of time to stress and to coerce through deadlines of all kinds. Let things be and let them evolve, thus strengthening respect for your own internal time clock. The real self must not be whipped or sacrificed through any mechanism or machination largely produced by society and inflicted by you or anyone else.

There are things that seem to need doing that do not need doing. There are changes we believe are necessary that are not necessary. Our procrastinations and avoidances are often indications that we really do not want to do things. In these cases resolutions and deadlines seldom activate us and only lead to self-hate. It is often constructive and a contribution to inner peace to accept these chronic delays as messages to ourselves and to give up attempts at forcing ourselves to do things, to complete things that we really do not want to do at all, ever.

17.

PRIORITIES, PROPORTION, PERSPECTIVE, AND APPROPRIATENESS

FORTUNATELY, MOST OF us can offer ourselves a "real timetable"—some kind of hierarchy of priorities based on *our* needs and preferences. Without priorities, living a life of relative inner peace in the middle of our complex, multipressured society would be impossible. But for most of us, the priorities we have exist only minimally on a conscious level; they have been imposed by outside standards, conventions, and pressures rather than being self-generated or consciously decided upon. If we make a *conscious* effort to establish a hierarchy of priorities, however, it can make a significant contribution to a life of greater inner peace and comfort.

Differentiating between *our priorities* and *society's shoulds* is of utmost importance since priorities make for self-mending and inner peace, while *shoulds* and the breaking of *shoulds* produce fragmentation, anxiety, self-hate, and stress. *Shoulds* and their partners, *should nots,* are rigid and unrelenting; they are often in conflict with each other; they are born of suffering rather than struggle; they feed pride, narcissism, self-glorification, and self-idealization. They are the fixed contracts society imposes on us, and breaking them leads to attacks of severe self-hate. Combined *shoulds* may be viewed as the equivalent of an overburdening, tyrannical, restrictive *conscience*, utterly destructive of free choice and dead to real inner needs. In Freudian terms these *shoulds* are the equivalent of a dictatorial, despotic superego. Each *should* requires satisfaction, and we cannot assign greater importance to one over another: all *shoulds* have instant and total priority over spontaneity and desires and actions born of real aliveness and needs. *Shoulds* resist an order of priority, since they all clamor for attention and satisfaction at the same time. This means that an attempt to satisfy one *should* immediately initiates a clamor from others and attacks of self-hate: you *should* buy your mother a birthday present and you *should* go to that meeting and you *should* get that research finished; and when you discover you can't do it all you feel you've failed. *Shoulds* may exist on a conscious level, but most often they operate from the unconscious, making for slavish behavior and misery whose origin is seldom traceable to the *should* by the victim. Likewise, the victim seldom knows that a *should* is a *should* and may very well believe that his needs to be perfect, lovable, helpful, masterful, or rich are born of real desire or priorities. If you want to fight this army of *shoulds*—and you'll have to, to win inner peace—you must set up a hierarchy of priorities, the antithesis of *shoulds* and the antidote for the stress of society's demands, temptations, and conflicts.

Choice and Individualism

Consciously struggling to develop one's own priorities is in itself a powerful exercise in self-realization. The desire for personal priorities is the desire for putting one's own feelings in the forefront of one's life. This is the stuff of real values, a personal style of life, a personal frame of reference, a real identity, and a significant contribution to spontaneity. As such, priorities are an excellent solvent for diluting and destroying both inner and outer coercions. They are a bulwark against thoughtless and feelingless conformity and resignation and surrender to cultural pressures antithetical to humanity and compassion for real self.

Priorities are the stuff of individuality; they fly in the face of automatic conformity and its blood brother, compulsive rebellion. And when you have set a reasonable hierarchy of priorities, you are flexible, not rigid: new conditions and considerations that come up in life can effect changes in your priorities and their position in the hierarchy, because when your values are based on priority, not on pride, your pride cannot be hurt. This removes slavish clinging to fixed positions inherent in *shoulds* and *should nots*. Indeed, the possibility of shifting, characteristic of real-self priorities, contributes to accommodation to new situations and to adaptability of almost infinite range. Adaptability is one of the great human characteristics that contribute to species survival. The freedom to establish and to change priorities is a superb cure for, and even more important, a prophylaxis against, all kinds of self-splitting conflicts, self-hate, and self-torture. Priorities negate conflict, and when changes necessitate new priorities, the ability to shift priorities continues to put off unnecessary conflict.

The fact is that having to choose between two alternatives becomes easier if we know where each alternative stands on our list of priorities. I am a doctor, and helping people is very high on my list of priorities: but I enjoy the things that money can buy as much as the next man. If I must choose between taking part in a potentially lucrative business transaction that will take bread out of someone else's mouth, and *not* taking part in the transaction (to my detriment), the choice is obvious. People matter more to me than money. If you don't know immediately where the alternatives stand, then the subsequent *struggle* to know will help in future assessments of the same or similar situations, because basic priorities will have been established. If you have priorities, you recognize the fact that a price must be paid, that all your desires and needs will not be satisfied. This alone is crucial to inner peace.

But in this matter of priorities I must make it clear that struggle for individual preferences cannot take place where there is capitulation to pride, glory, and success. Interest in true self and in self-realization in all aspects is the only climate in which real priorities can flourish. And we do not eventually arrive at a Mecca or ethereal plane that negates forever the need for further struggle. This struggle is a process and a way of life, a continuing adaptation to an ever-evolving encounter with life and reality.

To the extent that our priorities are based on real self they also help us see the real world—as well as our adaptation to it more clearly. This is so despite the fact that the world around us may be one of great rigidity and conformity, and of high destructive capacity. In the valley of the blind the sighted man may be seen as abnormal *but* he alone sees. Individuality and priorities born of individuality may very well make us different, but they will also make us more perceptive of our surroundings.

Importance and Self-Importance

Priorities, or *values*—as we may now also call them—give us a sense of appropriateness and proportion and perspective. They readily tell us what is and isn't important in our lives. This is very important in sustaining a solid sense of reality. Reacting to the hurts of pride positions destroys one's sense of reality and proportion. People live for their priorities. They seldom, if ever, die

or kill for them. But people often do kill for hurt pride
and for glory. I have seen men batter each other half to
death in highway arguments and in arguments over
parking spaces. These had nothing to do with priorities
but were the result of rage induced by hurt pride—pride
invested in confused macho notions and in the manifes-
tation of individual power. To die of a fractured skull
received in a fight over who is entitled to turn first is appropriate to pride/glorification/competition sickness. It
is inappropriate to the affirmation of life and self and
indicates a profound lack of perspective and sense of
proportion. This cannot happen to a person whose first
real priority is the preservation of life and self. His sense
of proportion, giving a very low priority to winning in
roadside confrontations, would enable him to acquiesce
without hurt feelings or any sense of personal debase-
ment or defeat.

Obviously a sense of proportion and appropriateness
is crucial to the maintenance of inner peace. Without
this sense we are subject to chronic onslaughts because
nearly all events in life are seen in a distorting mirror.

I remember driving with my father and wife. She was
driving the car. She made an error and turned on the
wrong street, two streets closer than the one for which
we were heading. My father suddenly screamed, "Oh,
my god!" I had been half asleep. I woke with a start.
She jammed on the brakes and we nearly went through
the windshield. She thought she had run over someone.
I thought he had had a heart attack. Neither was true.
He simply had realized that she turned up the wrong
block. Of course his reaction was inappropriate to the
event or the consequences. Our reaction to his reaction
could have been catastrophic. Fortunately it wasn't. But
was his reaction appropriate to anything? Yes, it was!
But not to a priority or to individuality or to self or to
reality. It was appropriate to a *should* and to pride:
pride in always being right and driving to the right place
without error; to the should: *you should not ever make
a mistake*. This *should* and pride is the stuff of per-

fectionism and self-glorification. It does not permit human treatment of self nor does it permit inner peace, since the possibility of error makes for the chronic threat of inappropriate and catastrophic reaction. Of course this is only a small example but we can see how this kind of inappropriateness, multiplied several hundred times, leads to chronic stress and lack of personal equanimity.

Of course, establishing real values and real priorities in lieu of pride is not a simple matter. It is part and parcel of working toward increased authenticity and dropping pretense and affectation generally. This is sometimes possible with self-examination, but those of us who are caught in a deep personal and cultural morass sometimes need outside help. In these cases, emotional and intellectual support from an insightful spouse or good friend can be helpful. Sometimes professional psychoanalysis is the way—but the therapist must not impose his *own* values and priorities on the patient. "Normal" *shoulds* are still *shoulds*. The analyst must resist the temptation to be too helpful. Otherwise the patient will suffer from the stifling effects of overprotection, which may have brought him into treatment in the first place, and he will adopt the analyst's standards as *shoulds*.

There are two practices which may be helpful to you in establishing real priorities: examining untoward reactions, and getting into the habit of stating personal preferences even if only to one's self.

Whenever we have an unusually strong or inappropriate emotional reaction—anxiety, anger, irritation, unhappiness—it behooves us to explore the possibility that we have, largely by habit or pride, attached too much importance to an event, person, or situation. (An example would be my father's overreaction to my wife's making a wrong turn on the road.) This enables us to establish or to reestablish a sense of appropriateness and to return the person or situation to its proper place in the order of personal priorities.

Setting Your Priorities

How can you do this? Stating personal preferences is
more than an act of self-assertion and affirmation of
self against self-effacement and compulsive compliancy.
It is also an identification of personal priorities, which
increases our feelings of personal substantiality.

Let me at this point list the entries in *my* hierarchy of
personal priorities. Your list might be longer or shorter,
and perhaps not as formalized—but making a list is an
especially good exercise with which to begin. Later on,
when you begin to absorb on a deep and emotional level
the relative value of various items in your life, formal
list-making becomes less necessary.

1) *Self.* Survival of the self, physically and emotionally,
comes first. Neglect of self and self-effacement are
enemies to the self. Lack of interest in others is also an
enemy of the self, but martyrdom for others is an affectation designed for pride and glory and is antithetical
to real self. And without real self, there is no way to
relate effectively to others.

The cornerstone of self-help is compassion for self.
This means living in a state of grace with one's self. This
means always forgiving one's self. It means never condemning one's self even as one remedies obvious wrongdoing on one's own part. It means absolute, constant,
unwavering loyalty to self. It means *never, never* abandoning one's self or ever joining an enemy of the self. It
means standing up to self-hate whenever it is encountered and in whatever form it takes: recrimination,
second-guessing, depression, self-deprecation, affectation, psychosomatic illness, suicide, "friendships" with
detractors, or other dangerous activity. I've detailed the
anatomy and physiology of compassion and self-hate in
the book by the same name.

2) *People* always receive priority over *things*, activities,
places, or any other aspects of life. This means that the

well-being of people is of first importance, and that any activity destructive of people is viewed with horror: deprivation of necessities on any level; sacrifice of people for material gain, power, prestige, cause, country, or ideal; stifling or discouraging the development of any person's proclivities, yearnings, interests, or growth.

Particular people receive top priority: family, friends, and children, one's own and others. Children and their welfare are of critical importance. Warmth in people and lack of affectation are of greater significance to me than charm.

A person's right to receive necessary care is not predicated on power, money, prestige, or contributions but rather on the immediacy and strength of the need. In other words, one realizes that each person is expected to give top priority to preservation of his or her own self and deserves aid in preserving that self.

3) *Feelings* take precedence over intellect, thought, and logic. Kindness and compassion toward self, toward others, and from others are of first priority. But, in keeping with the ancient saying, "Nothing human is alien to me," no feeling is unexpected, shunned, disregarded, deadened, or feared. This means that one expects and accepts all feelings without self-judgment or derision and one knows the difference between a feeling and an action. Feelings include: anger, loving, liking, jealousy, envy, rage, vindictiveness, possessiveness, fear, desire, joy, sorrow, depression, ecstasy, exhilaration, and the whole range of human emotions, including every conceivable blatant and subtle feeling and the innumerable mélanges of feelings.

We humans do not have separate, well-defined feelings. Our moods and feelings are confused because we often experience so many at the same time. Ambivalent feelings and constant shifts in feelings and moods are characteristic of us and to be compassionately expected. We are complex creatures, and respect for all that our

complexity entails is part of acceptance of ourselves and
other people as full participants in the human experience.

4) *Acceptance* of people as people takes precedence over
all social imperatives, including justice and the distribution of rewards and punishments. This means that part
of giving self and other people top priority is seeing
people in terms of people problems and people solutions. I certainly don't expect everyone to hold with this
priority but I do, and so I express it here. This means
that wrongdoing is viewed as maladaptive rather than as
volitional evil. It means that we must strain and struggle
to love those who are the least loved because their difficulties sometimes make them obnoxious, sometimes
dangerous, and often destructive.

They are hated because they are dangerous. But they
are often despised because they put us in touch with
aspects of ourselves that we fear. We must love the
human condition more than justice, more then vengeance, and enough to go beyond questions of guilt and
punishment. Even as we accept our own rage we must
accept the people we despise—enough to be able to seek
out the roots of their indiscretions and destructive
behavior and to pursue remedial measures rather than
punishment.

5) *Humility*. The toughest asset to come by is probably
the most valuable of all. I suppose humility is an attitude rather than a mood or a feeling. As I've already
indicated, it's the antipride agent and self-realizing
agent par excellence and is a top priority toward which
to work. Humility also makes it possible to learn, to
change, and to grow without investing undue pride in
fixed positions and in always being right.

6) *Style of life*—"doing one's thing," even if that choice
does not have either familial or conventional roots—has
high priority. This includes participating in an oc-

cupation that is appropriate to one's proclivities and that gives personal satisfaction.

7) *Creative enterprise* is quite high on this list. Satisfying one's own creative urges, as well as deriving pleasure from the work of others, is very important.

8) *Pleasure* (of course harmless and nondestructive) is of considerable importance, as is relative comfort or the state of being relatively free of anxiety.

9) *Aesthetics* is assigned a relatively high priority, but physical appearance does not come up beyond the low middle range.

10) *Humor* is very high on the list, as is laughter. But tears and the free expression of all emotions are just as high.

11) *Now, the present,* takes precedence over the past and the future. One is gone. The other is not yet here. We don't ignore either but there is no question at all that preference is given to the *here and now.* Thus, wherever possible, ruminations about the past, malignant nostalgia, and worries in anticipation of the future are curtailed and avoided. They are not permitted to impinge on real living, that which goes on *here and now.*

12) *Comfort* is important—as are material possessions, which contribute to comfort. *But* material possessions, including money, are not to be confused with blood, flesh, and life. Relative to life, *things of value* have no value. Ownership is not all-important. We can enjoy many things we see in museums, store windows, and in other people's homes without owning them. Adequate self-esteem usually removes the compulsive need to enhance and extend one's self through possession of adornments of all kinds. Since ownership of more things does not affect poor self-esteem, the quest for

relief through ownership of more and more becomes endless.

13) *Stress-free situations* are highly desirable, all things being equal. This means that if a choice is necessary and one option involves less stress than another, the stress-free option easily becomes the chosen one.

14) *People always come before principles.* I've already said this in different ways but it is so important that I want to state it again, clearly and simply. There is no contest between people and principles. People come first, last, and always! We are what the whole thing is all about.

15) *Security* has a low priority. We spend entirely too much of our time and energy destroying the present for the future in the service of security, which is largely an illusion. Security hardly exists at all. The human condition can be one of relative inner peace and emotional comfort but never one of security.

Insecurity is a prime characteristic of being human; knowing this and embracing it prevents disappointment, paralysis, and resignation. The quest for security is more than futile. It also destroys the desire, will, and ability to change and to grow.

Also of very low priority on this list are: being universally liked; admiration; being ahead of the others; power; prestige; always being right; bravery; any "macho" values (such as never needing help and always being in control); visions of love in which the lovers are seen as molding into one organism; and freedom from involvement and responsibility.

Once you're able to make a list of preferences, it is valuable to reassess periodically where you are and where you want to go. Many of us are inadvertently inundated by the everyday pressures of an extremely complicated world, and we tend to lose sight of who we really are and what has meaning and importance for us. It is important to take a close and objective look from time to time at how we are spending our lives. Sometimes, this is the only way to restore our sense of proportion and appropriateness.

Reassessment must not be confused with judgment. Its purpose is not to establish passing or failing grades but rather to restore, if necessary, a proper direction, or to help us change direction if we desire to do so. Principal priorities, which largely determine character structure and personality, tend to remain the same, although they can change too. But preferences in various areas may change with increased experience. Thus we may continue to give people the highest priority but may prefer to spend more time by ourselves. In any case periodic evaluation of our priorities will tell us which ones we may have been neglecting, and which ones we now feel we'd like to change.

I have seen a number of people over the years who became depressed because, without their awareness, their priorities had been eroded. They came to feel that their lives were meaningless. Treatment largely consisted of reestablishing their values and thus restoring meaning and self-esteem in their lives.

18.

UNTHINK

IN SETTING PRIORITIES, what we *feel* is more important than what we *think*. I have come to believe that most thinking is destructive! There are still signs on desks which issue the command THINK! I would prefer signs which read THINK LESS or UNTHINK! I believe that a great deal of the mind-verbalizing or thinking that we do constitutes a major and chronic disturbance to inner peace.

Let me caution at once that my suggestion to exercise the process of not thinking or what we may call *unthink* is in no way an argument for impulsive action of any kind. Indeed, excess thinking often leads to impulsive acting out. This occurs because overthink (and overthink is the process most of us are caught in) so paralyzes us that explosive acting out is often the destructive method we use to break through inertia.

I am not against appropriate thinking and the use of logic and reason. Unfortunately our society has blown up the use of logic and thinking to malignant proportions. Thus thinking has become *overthink* and overthink has metastasized into areas of our being where it ought to be exercised minimally.

The degree of verbal excess is truly astounding. This is evidenced in useless verbosity in so-called business meetings, speeches of all kinds, writing of all kinds, social situations, teaching, and, most important of all, in one's own head.

Unfortunately, much of the intellectualizing is damaging to productive or creative thinking and enterprise. Overthink is mainly used to obfuscate real meaning and feelings; to manipulate others and self; as an extension of repressed desires and feelings; as an attempt to handle anxiety; as an avoidance mechanism in evading real issues and actions; as a duplicitous gesture and affectation; as harassments of self to the detriment of inner peace, emotional integrity, and emotional availability, that is, accessibility to feelings.

How many conversations I have listened to in which the information conveyed was in inverse proportion to the number of words emitted. Unfortunately the same is true of talks with ourselves, in our own heads. So much of our own intrapsychic verbal activity is used for all kinds of obfuscation. Unfortunately, much of it is also used as a form of ruminative worry and planning and delaying and paralyzing—often as a process of self-hate.

The effect of overthink or ututoverbalization is the destruction of real communication, especially that involving feelings, who we really are, and who and what we really value and live for. It is interesting to note how few words are necessary when we really have something to say and really want to say it so that the other person will understand. I am reminded of Einstein and Camus, who had so much to say and said it so succinctly.

The same is true in conveying meaning of consequence and substance to ourselves. The effect of a word- or think-glut is to fragment, to repress, and to create general chaos in the mind so as to obfuscate. One ultimate effect of overthink is exhaustion. But its most destructive effect is to put its victim out of touch with the mainstream of himself. The thought processes are for all intents and purposes split off from the real substance of the individual. The thinking takes on an autonomy of its own, creating a powerfully divisive and distracting diversion.

In cases, and there are many, where overthink is strong and runs rampant, the feeling self—the self of richness, of creativity, and of authenticity—is all but lost in the shadow of the thinking process. Unfortunately, much that we are called upon to do in the everyday world feeds this ascendancy of thinking, of words, over feelings.

Words are symbols and can be very valuable in abstract thinking and in arriving at constructive insights and conclusions. But *overthink* to me represents what we may call *symbol sickness*. This is a condition in which a greater and greater distance grows between the symbol and what it represents. Eventually, the symbol or word is almost entirely removed from its original representation and loses almost all meaning on a feeling level. In this way thinking becomes autonomous, takes on a life of its own, and becomes its own reason for being. It distracts and uses up energy and time that might otherwise be used fruitfully. It also creates confusion, procrastination, inhibition, and paralysis. This is so because anything that cuts us off from our mainstream and hinders our being in touch with our feelings is a blow to integration and to spontaneity, which are necessary to fruitful movement and action.

We usually consider thought given to environmental demands as constructive in producing action. But this is often not the case. Thinking, especially excess thinking, is often used as a substitute for action. Even worse, thinking that produces distance from real self prevents effective action, because action is largely a function of integrity and availability of feelings. How can we do what we want if we don't know what we want? How can we know what we want if we are preoccupied with thinking about what we want instead of *feeling what we want*?

I feel that there is entirely too much *thinking consideration* given to too many things. Most *doing* simply does not require thinking, or at most requires minimal thinking. I remember spending hours and hours devising a plan to study. The planning to study, actually a form of *overthink*, resulted in absolutely no increase of my knowledge in the subjects I needed and wanted to learn. As my planning and thinking went on I got more and more caught up in it. It began to take on an importance of its own. The study plan and the subject *it* covered and the time *it* would use began to have less and less to do with *me*. *I* and my original purpose—to learn important material—were left out of it. Then the pressure began to build. Time was growing short and I had learned little or nothing. I was still busy planning. More important, *I*, the real *I* that wanted to learn, was being starved by my increasing inertia. I suddenly realized that I was caught in a morass of thinking, worrying, planning, and anticipating. Consciousness of the problem and a direct act of will extricated me from this destructive diversion. I no longer planned to study and never did again. I realized that the doing was infinitely more important than the thinking about doing and that the latter could in no way be a substitute for the former. I also realized that thinking was not necessary as a prelude to study even though it takes place as an intrinsic part of the study process itself. How did I do it? I did it by doing it! This is not a play on words. I simply dropped any thinking or planning, went directly to a book (any of several I had to study) and started to read and to struggle to understand the substance of the work I was *doing*. I refused even to think which book ought to come first. It just didn't matter enough to think about it since I wanted to learn all the subjects eventually.

I had made an important discovery for myself, a discovery that is applicable in many areas. *Most doing* does not require thinking and *all doing requires doing*.

In this connection I want to say that *mindless activity* is a valuable exercise and can be restful, peace enhancing, and restorative. Walking with minimal thinking is excellent, as is knitting and weaving or hitting golf balls (not in competition with self or others) or just sitting. It is not easy to empty the mind of words and thought. But with practice this can be done relatively, although not absolutely. I do not care for contrivances such as repetition of a mantra or the application of quasimystical modalities. I much prefer the application of insight and the development of individual activities designed for mindlessness or thoughtlessness. The very business of trying to extend our doing-without-thinking—to do more and more thoughtless doing—is a very helpful exercise, and the entire process gets easier as we practice it. All of us actually do a great deal without verbal intervention— brush our teeth, eat, and so forth—so it is not as if we completely lack experience in this area. As children we do many things without thinking, but as we grow older society impinges upon us. If we allow ourselves to become conscious of these impingements, to become conscious of *overthink*, we have a much better chance of dissipating this block to spontaneity, and extricating ourselves from anxiety and depression.

19.

HERE AND NOW

AWARENESS OF THE stressful destructiveness of our culture, desire for peaceful reconciliation of ourselves with ourselves, and knowledge of the path we must follow to extricate ourselves from the thickets of anxiety are only the beginning of the way to inner peace. To *live* what we *know*, we must begin with practical steps; and I offer these here-and-now exercises as first steps along the road.

Proofs, dares, challenges, and tests: Avoid them—whether they're as minor as an extra game of tennis you're roped into, or as major as taking on the responsibility of an enormous new house that you're not sure you can afford. If they can't be avoided, approach them with caution and a very big grain of salt. They are usually competition-derived devices and enemies to self and to reconciliation into mainstream cohesiveness. Don't be goaded into proofs and tests of intelligence, bravery, strength, purity, willpower, sexuality, endurance, or niceness.

Opening closures to goodness: Make a list of areas of your life and activities that you have somehow closed to goodness; work on opening them up.

I asked one man to do just that. The following is his list of "denials to goodness":

Closure to taking the best possible care of my health and my one and only life. This applies to eating sensibly and exercising regularly.

The joy of making music. I used to enjoy playing the violin and the piano, and conducting.

The enjoyment of sex and having a good time with my wife.

Simply being in a good mood.

Satisfaction from writing and other forms of self-expression.

Feelings of warmth from more direct exchanges of feelings with people. I have inadvertently allowed myself to become increasingly reserved and much too detached and isolated over the years. Waiting for people to approach me after I've rejected them for years won't work. Perhaps I can approach them.

Satisfaction from tackling problems and tasks instead of self-torturing procrastinating, but without a sense of obligation.

The good feeling derived from experiences, excursions, theater, reading, and having just plain fun.

Satisfaction from involvement with my job.

Satisfaction from expressing my feelings and opinions.

The joy of laughter.

Pride traps and tickles: Many situations come up that tempt us in pride areas or, as my analyst, Nat Freeman, used to say, "tickle our pride." These can trap us into long-standing stressful situations, which we really don't want. I remember being unexpectedly offered an opportunity to teach a course in Freudian theory at the Analytic Institute many years ago. This was unusual because I was very young, especially in terms of my connection to the institute. Of course my pride was "tickled"—pride in being smart enough to be asked, pride in prestige, and pride in being academically ahead of colleagues who started ahead of me. I accepted immediately with hardly any consideration at all of whether I wanted to prepare for the course, or whether I wanted to teach week after week for fifteen weeks. I spent a miserable summer preparing for the course, dropping other activities I really had in mind and wanted to do. Teaching the course was even worse. Extricating myself from teaching the course the following year was even more difficult. I have learned to be wary of accepting pride temptations since that time.

Pleasing others, applause, and prizes: These play an enormous role in our society. To please others is fine if at the same time we please ourselves. Admiration, kudos, and prizes are nice if they are given for things we really want to do. But pleasing others to the detriment of self and seeking admiration by excluding real needs are highly destructive. Decisions and activities that are functions of the attempt to be nice and to be universally liked serve a brutal taskmaster who cares nothing about the self. Striving for prizes easily becomes a ruthless addiction that impoverishes the self. These are antithetical to inner well-being and must not be substituted for day-to-day personal living, which brings peaceful comfort even if it does not bring admiration.

Wants: To want something (and I differentiate here between want and need—I mean to want something that you do not need at all) is wonderful. To want it is a good feeling and to satisfy that desire is good. But to become a slave of any want destroys inner peace. To collect stamps, watches, coins can be fun and to want particular items and to wait for them with pleasant anticipation is fine. But to become trapped into stressful living by wants and things is to relegate the self to a subservient, sacrificial position. If wants are very strong it behooves us to satisfy them, but at the same time to evaluate them in a real frame of reference so as to protect the primacy of the self.

Pretentious acts: A woman I know—call her Myra—"sat on her smartness" when she went out with Dan because she did not want to threaten him. Dan became her husband—and for twenty-five years she muted her vitality and intelligence to "make it easy on him." She grew to hate herself in the process, and to hate him also. When we begin to dissemble, most of us are almost always aware of it. We must exert willpower and stop ourselves as soon as we recognize that we are acting falsely. No other person must be allowed to force us into pretending to be what we are not. This is the epitome of self-hate and invariably leads to destruction of inner unity and peace of mind.

Comparisons: Beware of comparisons. Most of them are odious and are functions of pride-oriented competition. We usually compare ourselves and our various situations in life with ideals we wish to achieve in order to prod ourselves on in endless Sisyphean labors. If we must make comparisons, it is self-saving to use standards of reality and not fantasy. In this connection it is good to remember that a price must be paid for everything. If I compare my financial status with that of a rich businessman, I must ask, Do I want to spend my life in pursuit of dollars? Do I want to surrender the time I spend doing the many enjoyable things I do for myself now?

Self-assertion: The value of self-assertion has been grossly exaggerated in our society—and self-assertion has been confused with aggression. We do not put the next fellow down when we really assert ourselves—that is aggression. Also, forcing ourselves to assert ourselves when we do not feel like it is actually an act of compliance. In this case we comply with a *should* or inner dictate even as we act out assertively with someone else. This is a pretense and is destructive to self. Self-assertion is valuable when it is natural and when its consequences are constructive. To be hurt or killed or to hurt or put down others in the service of assertion is not a function of self but rather a function of sick pride.

Twenty-five common coronary compulsions: I call these *coronary compulsions* because these "needs," which aren't needs at all, are the stuff of coronary occlusions or heart attacks. These no-need "needs" (we don't need them at all) work in the service of pride-connected *shoulds* and run rampant in our culture. I've already described a few of them. This is the list. Instant recognition of them and a struggle against them wherever and whenever they appear can be lifesaving and therefore self-saving, too.

1) The need to be loved.
2) The need to be admired.
3) The need to be right.
4) The need to be brilliant.
5) The need to convince others of ideas, opinions.
6) The need to win, to be first, the most, the best.
7) The need to be needed and to be missed when not present.
8) The need to understand everything.
9) The need to be in charge, on top of all situations.
10) The need to be in control of all of one's emotions at all times.
11) The need to attain security.
12) The need for respect.
13) The need always to be able to assert oneself, regardless of circumstances.
14) The need to get things accomplished and done. There's a great difference between "I must do it" and "I'd like to do it."
15) The need for perfection in any area.

16) The need for status—any and all kinds.
17) The need to stay young, beautiful, athletically competent, talented.
18) The need for ownership.
19) The need to know the future.
20) The need always to be helpful, always to be charitable, always to share. This often takes the form of not being able to give oneself a desired item until everyone else in the family has it also.
21) The need for perfect, everlasting health.
22) The need always to be happy, never to be sad, never to be anxious, to sustain no mood fluctuations.
23) The need to be free of any kind of irritation.
24) The need never to sustain any frustration or pain of any kind.
25) The need always to sustain perfect integrity and truth. This is sometimes carried to the point of destruction of oneself as well as others. It sometimes results in the countercompulsive reaction of utter ruthlessness and disregard for truth and integrity to the point of chronic, compulsive lying.

Fantasy tragedy and real tragedies: Real tragedies—a death, or a serious loss—are inevitable, and our response to them is appropriate sadness. But continued, eternal sadness is inappropriate even in the case of the most severe loss. Facing the fact of inevitability and struggling against happy-ever-after expectations is helpful. Incapacitating, unrelenting tragic response is not evidence of true or deep love as much as it is evidence of morbid dependency, rejection of the limitations inherent in being human, and self-dramatization. Creating tragedy where there is none—when you have lost your job, but there are others to be had, or losing $50,000 when you have $5,000,000—and exaggerating tragic events are often masochistic attempts at stimulation for synthetic aliveness. These produce serious stress, however, and are blocks to real pleasure, peace of mind, and reality orientation.

Helplessness must and will occur at times. Accepting it and getting necessary help is evidence of humility and maturity. Acceptance means, of course, no recriminations and self-hate at all, and no embarrassment or self-hate projected onto the helper.

A man I know has a favorite saying, "No good deed goes unpunished." Unfortunately, this is often the case —crippled people hate their crutches—largely because of inability to accept help. Accepting help and giving help, the essence of cooperation, get easier with practice and are of great therapeutic value. May I say in this connection that cooperation often takes the form of serious listening and talking in which real feelings are conveyed. It takes exercise and practice to be open to, to accept, to appreciate, and to enjoy other people's caring. Unfortunately, many of us suffer from cynicism and downright paranoia and don't recognize the real thing when it is presented. We become suspicious, react with hurt pride and even rage. To practice openness to the possibility of real caring is the essence of relating cooperatively and perhaps the very best of being human.

Physical self: The everyday care of physical self is crucial. It includes healthy eating with attention to what one enjoys eating and with whom and when. Individual appetites must not be ignored even as the usual nutritional characteristics of various types and amounts of food are considered. Good and appropriate exercise, especially of an enjoyable kind, is valuable. Good sex is valuable. Enjoyable work is crucial. Ample sleep appropriate to individual needs is very important; one must not struggle to sleep a prescribed length of time. Relaxation, play, and fun are urgent and are real needs, especially here and now in our society. It is important to know when we are tired and to do something about it so as not to exceed our physical limits and not to deplete our physical selves in heroic gestures of any kind.

Nostalgia: This is a heartfelt and warm emotion or mood but it behooves us not to get caught up in chronic obsession with the past. It is especially important not to depreciate the *here and now* by making odious comparisons with an imagined, modified, and exaggerated past that never could have existed. This is often done in the service of self-hate and prodding oneself on for greater glory.

Hate: Hatred usually represents projected areas of self-hate. This means that work must be done to seek out what it is we hate in ourselves so as to struggle to encompass it, to increase self-acceptance, and to mitigate rage at others on whom we project the hated characteristics.

Vacations: Vacations have value, emotionally and physically, only if we are ready to take them, and if they are the kind *we want*. To go to Europe just because everyone is doing it and "it is the thing to do"—when you hate to travel or are afraid of foreign places—will only produce stress. The same is true of honeymoons, cultural events, social situations, and all forms of entertainment and participation in sports. Complying with so-called cultural norms and peer pressures can be disastrous to self.

Motivation to do and especially to do in the service of change is infinitely more rewarding if it springs from happiness rather than unhappiness. It is valuable to break the habit of waiting for dissatisfaction and unhappiness as motivations for change and growth. We can seek out new areas and look for changes even while we are content with old ones and the status quo. Some people artificially depreciate who they are, what they have, and where they are, so as to be able to make changes without a sense of loss. This maneuver produces most important losses in terms of self-esteem and reality. It also makes for discontent and restlessness and the feeling of not taking oneself seriously enough to be honest with oneself. The reality is that it is easier to accommodate to change from a position of strength, a situation with which one is happy. Depreciation of the status quo weakens us and makes accommodation to changes more difficult and often quite painful as well.

Money: Periodic reassessment of money is a good way of combating the money/status syndrome. It means reviewing the fact that money is best used as a means of exchanging time and energy. Money is a convenient expedient and ought not be a slave-maker. There are many factors about which I am not in the least expert, but two considerations are very important to me. The first is that an investment must not create undue stress. The second, a corollary of the first, is that no investment is permitted to conflict with my priorities or style of life. This means, for example, that I would in no way participate in an enterprise in which I would be a slumlord. Likewise, I would sell my house if I wanted to live in another one, but I would not sell it to live in a small apartment in order to have the money to make more money. This is in accordance with my priorities. A businessman may have a different viewpoint entirely in this last regard.

Coping with it all: As problems come up in our lives we can cope with *some* of them. It is important to emphasize to ourselves that *we can't cope with them all*, much less at the same time. Throughout life there are many times when our ability to cope is minimal and even nonexistent. Some problems will never be resolved and some will never go away. Others will be eroded by time itself. Coping with coping, that is, relative equanimity about coping, is increasingly valuable in our complex, disturbed society.

Obsessive opportunism: Obsessive opportunism—always sending out a résumé when you hear of a job opening, whether you're happy in your present job or not—is often seen as appropriate behavior in our society but is certain death to the self. Periodic assessment of all activities, including social involvement, is valuable in assessing whether or not real-self values are being satisfied or ruthlessly ignored. It is also wise to be wary of other people's exhortations about seizing "obvious opportunities." These can turn out to be *pride tickles* working in the service of pride opportunism to the detriment of self.

The status quo and personal responsibility: Whenever we complain to ourselves or to others about the situation we find ourselves in, we must tackle the following insight. The status quo, any and all aspects of our current situation, is largely, if not always completely, of our own making. Therefore, *we* can change it. This is consistent with and supports the belief that man has escaped instinct dictates and that he is much more than an instinct-driven mechanism. Knowing this is necessary before a real change can be made. Otherwise we continue to feel that change can take place only as a result of powers outside ourselves, and paralysis, frustrations, rage, and self-hate ensue.

Time: Many situations can be clarified only by the passing of time. Tearing, pushing, and pulling seldom lead to acceleration in situations requiring evolvement and development. But they do lead to self-depletion. *Take your time* (and that means "take time," and make it "your" time—not someone else's).

The unbeautiful and deadening: While I do not suggest that we seek out the grotesque in life, I feel that it is important not to deaden our sensibilities and to attempt to create a false fantasy world of beauty by shutting our eyes to harsh realities. When I walk down Third Avenue in New York City I do see much dirt in the street and the air could be much better too. I don't deaden myself to it. I see it all as part of this city's life and I choose to live and to work here as part of my own priorities. There are times when I choose to leave for a while and to experience country-clean beauty. But for the most part I choose the city and this means all of it—no exemptions, no needless complaints. I do what I can and live fully alive with the full aliveness of the city. Under the grime I see the beauty of the buildings. Because I don't deaden myself I enjoy the people, the stores, the food smells, and even the sky when it can be seen.

The discovery of ignorance in ourselves or in others is not evidence of stupidity or cause for embarrassment or derision. Ignorance is evidence that an area of knowledge has, for whatever reason, been ignored. This gives an opportunity to learn and to grow, to become involved, and to have new interests. Real humility may even welcome ignorance with joy for the anticipation of learning pleasure that it may bring.

Geographical and occupational changes: These changes are sometimes necessary and even lifesaving to people who cannot otherwise extricate themselves from high-stimulation temptations or rat-race occupations. If you have a high-pressure advertising job in a big city and find that, no matter how hard you try, you cannot slow down and ease the stress out of your life, you may well have to consider quitting the job and moving away from the city. If you stay—even if you find an ostensibly less competitive job—you may find you still have the compulsion to be a big fish in a big pond. And the quality of your real life will suffer. If you can't change the size of the fish (you), you can at least change the size of the pond. *There is nothing wrong with being a big fish in a small pond*—or a small fish in any pond.

Pleasure and rewards: You should not dole out pleasure to yourself as a reward for "accomplishment" of any kind, any more than you should inflict punishment for so-called "failures." Pleasure, however we attain it, is excellent therapy and must be applied without regard for "deserving it" or "working for it." It must be considered as a human prerogative. Real pleasure, by definition, cannot involve destructive effects on either self or others, because it works in tandem with self-realization.

Surrender and retreat: No matter what the circumstances, it is important to learn to "take the count," to sound retreat, to surrender without self-hate. It is often lifesaving, and our lives are more important than any single issue. With sufficient humility and life experience, we learn when surrender is inevitable. Pride destroys this ability, and since many defeats are inevitable, each defeat destroys our well-being if we sustain the pride position. Attempting to do the impossible is not constructive. It is defeating, depleting, and stressful. Being able to differentiate the impossible from the possible is evidence of the healthiest and most self-preservative kind of judgment. With ample humility and experience we "roll with the punches" and are freed of the myopic cultural vision of defeat and success.

Decision blocks: If, in a particular issue, a decision cannot be made, look for remedy in the following areas; they often exist unconsciously.
1) Lack of ability to surrender.
2) Unwillingness to pay a price.
3) Lack of enough mulling over mainly on a nonthink, unconscious, "let it perk" level.
4) Undeveloped priorities.
5) Consider that some situations don't require decisions at all and our inability to make a decision may be an indication that we really desire to leave the situation as is.

People's limitations: It is vital to learn to live with people's limitations, especially our own. However expert a person is in any area of endeavor, we cannot hope to get the impossible from him. There may be times when he can't even deliver what is possible. Since we are human, limitations are not only there, they are also in a constant state of flux relative to feelings, moods, and many other factors that affect us. To expect the impossible of people, and that includes expectation of consistently fine performance, is to court disappointment, anger, and inner stress and turmoil.

Serious business can be fun if you avoid every kind of overextension in terms of money, control (inability to delegate to other people), and self-importance. That serious activity *remains* fun is crucial to well-being.

Protection against arrogance, projections, and claims: People will at times certainly make neurotic claims on us, be arrogant to us, be unconsciously angry with us and project their difficulty onto us. To react with hurt pride, to get into pride deadlocks, to attempt to win and to score with vindictive triumph, and to withdraw compulsively are almost always self-damaging and destructive to the relationship, which for the most part may be worthwhile.

If necessary, remove yourself from the scene of such conflicts for a short time. Of course the ultimate protection comes out of the realization that we are all separate entities with separate autonomies and separate problems. The individual doing the projecting may not realize this, but you, the self-protector, must. The second step is to try to understand the nature of his or her problem: What is it that the person won't face in himself or herself and is projecting? What is the underlying fear causing the arrogance? What is the internal compulsive *should* which has now become a claim on others? The third step is to realize that the person has a problem that you may or may not be able to help with, largely depending on the degree of openness and the desire to be helped. The fourth and crucial step is not to personalize—that is, to realize this is another person's problem, and that you don't need to react to it.

In this connection I must point out—and this is not a sanctimonious or angelic attitude; it is practical—that finding what is good and worthwhile in other people, even when they are neurotically unfair, helps rid you of anger and promotes tranquillity.

The day's textures: By texture of the day I mean the mood we are in and the feelings we have at a particular time—how the world looks and feels to us on any given day. To the extent that we know how we feel and how the world feels to us, and that we can live the day in peace, in keeping with our feelings, we are not violating the texture. Living each day relative to that "texture," as much as possible, is the essence of going along with self and being mellow. This is the process of reconciling our activities and the outside world to our moods.

Options and compulsivity: In issues where we have several options or possibilities, we have greater freedom of choice if we can remove the compulsive feelings we may have about each option. We don't *have* to do anything. This means removing the emotional input and diluting the emotional investment of each choice.

Fun and seriousness: It is urgent that we realize that having fun and being serious are not inconsistent. Also being somber and solemn is in no way evidence of being serious. Also being relaxed is not evidence of lack of application of effort or struggle.

Creating a scene: Fear of creating a "scene," used as an inhibition to express anger, is destructive to mellow living and reconciliation of emotional vectors in ourselves. People can become comfortable with "scenes" with practice.

Problems and time off: It is very valuable to realize that we can take time off from problems and come back later on to deal with them. They will still be there. Practicing makes it easier to do this. We can learn to "put things aside," to make them wait—while we rest.

Instant adaptations: You simply cannot adapt instantly to new situations; acclimatizations of any kind require time. This applies to good situations and even excellent ones, as well as to poor ones. Of course this especially applies to new relationships.

Games: If you treat bridge games, golf, poker, or tennis appropriately, without a sense of real competition, if winning at them does not represent a pride investment but continues to be for fun, then they can be therapeutic. Otherwise you might seriously consider quitting. Sometimes it helps to *play* with a different group. A game is often an excellent kind of Rorschach-like projective microcosm in which to learn about people and their underlying motivation.

"In the service of what?": This is an excellent question to ask ourselves about any given behavior or action. Had I asked myself this question before I consented to teach the Freud course, I might have saved myself much stress and difficulty. I might have realized that I consented not in the service of self, not because of interest in Freud or in teaching, but rather in the service of pride. The service of self often involves tapping our inner resources with real satisfaction in the use and evolvement of self. Pride and image seldom make constructive use of real resources and are often connected to duplicity and manipulation of self and others.

No: Learning to say *no* to any entanglements and activities that are stress-producing and can be avoided gets easier with practice. Temptations may be difficult to resist initially. This is to be expected. But it does get easier. When offered a proposition, any proposition at all, buy time before consenting to it. One way is to say, "Let me mull it over for a few days." Another is to ask for a written request or proposal, in the case of telephone communications. This is especially important for people who have a history of compliance and an inability to say no. Many people make impulsive decisions in order to avoid conflict or—as one of my patients puts it—"to get straightened out right away, no loose ends." The same man confused impulse with feelings. Impulsive decision-making and acting out destroy the possibility of development and evolvement of feelings.

New responsibilities: Taking on any responsibility, no matter how minor, requires ample consideration; don't offer to do something out of "nice guy" compulsive compliance, or as a grandstanding gesture, or as response to any kind of *pride tickle*. We all have limits and going beyond them invites strain and stress.

Greatness: It is helpful and interesting periodically to reevaluate our feelings of admiration for people we think of as great. Are they glory-seekers, warriors, omnipotent statesmen? Are they humanitarians? If our heroes have imperfections, perhaps we can allow ourselves some, too. Be wary of all idealizations—those that apply to yourself, your friends, and distant heroes.

Am I doing what I want or what I should?: This is a good question to ask ourselves to determine if we are freely in charge of ourselves or compulsive slaves in the service of inner tyranny.

Trying it: You are free to try any activity or relationship to determine how you feel about it. You need make only a *minimal* emotional investment until your feelings have evolved more fully—and this also, of course, means no *pride investment* at all.

Wrong and right: There are times when doing what is wrong, practically and on principle—telling a white lie, for example—is right because it is kinder. This again depends on priorities and values.

Enjoy less than the best: We've become a society of severe critics in almost all areas of life. This destroys enjoyment and inner peace. A movie, a book, a meal, and nearly all aspects of life can be less than perfect and can still be enjoyable, satisfying, and useful. Perfectionistic demands are antithetical to the human condition and killers of personal equanimity.

Living happily ever after: No one lives happily ever after! Knowing this is crucial in avoiding disappointment and inner turbulence.

Contempt: It is important to see if we have contempt for anyone and to clarify our feelings. Are they projected aspects of self? Are they influenced by cultural dictums?

Constructive "tests": No test of ourselves, whether it is running in a marathon or taking a college entrance exam, should be undertaken if it doesn't help us to develop our selves.

Hospitalization: If you're tired and worn down, you can help to avoid hospitalization by lying back and permitting others to take care of you.

Good deals: No deal is a good deal, however profitable it is, if we are not up to doing it and if it is antithetical to self-realization and personal priorities.

A small list of illusions to give up in the search for inner peace:

1) That we can have it all.

2) That there are "good guys and bad guys" rather than mixtures and people to whom we can relate well or poorly as the case may be.

3) That there is no time for self (even though we believe that time is endless, that we live forever).

4) That physical limits do not exist and that changes do not occur or that they can be postponed indefinitely.

5) That old yearnings disappear completely and that resolutions of conflicts can take place completely.

6) That security can be attained.

7) That we can completely control our immediate worlds and fates (even though we believe that we have little or nothing at all to say about our lives).

8) That we are the most important subject of everyone else's lives and attention.

9) That one day we will grow up completely.

10) That we or anyone else can know it all.

11) That most issues have well-delineated "rights" or "wrongs."

Strong feelings: Don't feel upset if you are made anxious by initial contact with formerly deadened feelings. Any increased aliveness, any feelings that are unfamiliar, can be anxiety-producing. As we have the experience of stronger and stronger feelings anxiety disappears.

Duty investments: These are activities of any kind that we do out of a sense of duty. If this "sense" gives us well-being, the activity can be constructive in terms of self. But many of these activities (for example, entertaining people we don't like) are actually compliance with "shoulds" and destructive to the self and its integrity.

Range of adaptability: Adaptation takes time and struggle. But we must not underestimate our ability to adapt. Most of us are much more adaptable than we think we are.

Telling secrets: I am talking here of revealing secrets about oneself as an exercise in being increasingly open. Periodically tell yourself how you feel about each person you know and when you can, tell them also. Telling them that you care, that you love them gets easier with practice.

Uncluttering: Uncluttering your life of thinking, blaming others, complaining, resolving, and planning can be of enormous help in making you open to goodness.

Vindictive triumph fantasies are better avoided if possible. They are ultimately destructive of inner peace and represent capitulation to a pride position.

Capitulation to enjoyment represents a struggle for a lot of people, but it is a most worthwhile one.

Beware of cultural wisdom: To breast feed or not to breast feed; to let baby cry or to pick up and cuddle; to study or not to study math and Latin as mind sharpeners. One's own judgment must never be ignored.

20.

RECONCILIATION TO DEATH AND THE CELEBRATION OF LIFE

WHEN WE HAVE made all possible reconciliations in our lives—with ourselves, with others, with the world as it is—there is one final and most important reconciliation to be made. Unless reconciliation to death takes place, at least to a relative degree, we cannot celebrate life.

All of us learn about death early in life and then we either repress the subject or we face it. But if we don't reconcile ourselves to death one or more of several possibilities takes place.

We may spend our lives devising and acting out stratagems and defenses to avoid confrontations with it. These include all kinds of health-fad beliefs and practices; religious beliefs and practices constructed to provide heavens in which we will continue to live forever; beliefs in magic and spiritualism of all kinds; comforting beliefs such as: "Aren't we all part of the same genetic pool and species? If any human being remains alive after me, then in a way I'm alive, too." This especially applies to children: "After all, they have my genes; they will be my living representatives here on earth after I die. Therefore it won't be as if I'm dead at all since I'll be alive through them. They will even contain and carry memories of me.''

We may become anxious as a result of conscious or unconscious awareness of this real human limitation and our inability to alter it. This anxiety produces chaos; it destroys inner peace and the celebration of life. It also makes us invest still more heavily in stratagems. If the anxiety is severe enough, one's whole life becomes a series of obsessive constructs to avoid and magically to negate the reality of inevitable death.

Humility, so necessary to well-being, is destroyed by still more stratagems of the "grand gesture" variety. These include the accumulation of money, estates, businesses, and so forth, which are unconsciously seen as immortal institutions through which we will live on even after our death. We construct all kinds of monuments to ourselves: collections of all kinds, creative works to live after us, pyramids, and whole cemeteries. During our lives we stratify our immediate society into all kinds of hierarchies based on money, power, beauty, fame in an attempt to convince ourselves that we have God-like dimensions and have transcended mortality after all.

But these very devices indicate that even in life, in not reconciling ourselves to the inevitability of death, we are death's slaves. If our energy, much like that of the pharaohs but on a subtler, more duplicitous level, is directed by our reaction to death, we cannot be free to live and indeed have unwittingly dedicated our lives to death. To the extent, and it is relative, that we struggle for reconciliation to death, we struggle for humility, humanity, inner peace, and life.

For myself, the belief that life and death are separate is a short-sighted view. In the long view, life and death are brothers in eternity.

I am not at all certain that the fear of death is natural to our species. I am sure that much of the fear and the sense of insult and ensuing rage are generated by our society or culture. I am also sure that the love of life does not lead to a fear of death, nor is the fear of death evidence of love of life. The culture creates much difficulty by its investment in pride in youth; disrespect and disregard of the aged; lack of humility and reality with regard to the human condition; pride in omnipotence; and lack of respect for other forms of life on this planet, for nature, and for the universe, *the whole of it*, of which we are a part.

Our society, with its pride-driven, competitive, "mind your own business" philosophy, unwittingly promotes a peculiar narcissism that extends the fear and insult of death, since death is the ultimate defeat for the seeker after glory. But narcissism does more than that. When narcissism causes disregard for *the whole of it*, it separates the narcissist from the rest of the world. The narcissist becomes his own world and believes the whole world is him. And yet even as he continues to strive in the service of this self-preoccupation (the antithesis of self-realization), he is conscious of the universe, and he feels the separation of himself from the *whole* of it—the separation he has been creating—and this very separation terrifies him. Relative to eternity he is so small. *But* if we feel ourselves part of humanity, and struggle accordingly for human values and humility, if we feel humanity as part of eternity, then life and death are indeed brothers in eternity. And we, as part of life and death and eternity, suffer no separations and no sense of the crush of eternity. Although we feel so small we also feel big, because we are part of the whole and the whole is very big.

I find it a comfort to know that the world will go on without me, and therefore I have no illusions at all that that small consciousness known as *me* must survive so that the world will go on. I am not the world or the universe, only part of it, and therefore my responsibility is limited.

Reconciliation to death permits the celebration of that phase or condition we call life. Walt Whitman wrote, "I celebrate myself," and I like that line. I believe that we can celebrate life and we can enjoy the failure or success of it, the joy, fun, sadness, nostalgia—life in all of its ramifications. This life as a human being is a superb opportunity for celebration. Reconciliation to all human realities, death included, aids the celebration.

PART III

*QUESTIONS AND
ANSWERS ON
RECONCILIATION AND
ANXIETY*

I have been asked a number of questions by people who have read the manuscript. In this section I try to answer these questions and to anticipate others, as well as to deal with questions that have come up in my own mind while working on the book.

I also hope that this section will serve as an exercise or a kind of practice experience in mellow feeling and thinking. If it does, perhaps readers will have more questions, and will design their own individual answers.

Does perception of the world change as we become increasingly mellow or reconciled?

Yes, time moves more slowly. The environment is less harsh. Rain, snow, odors, broken streets are seen and experienced with greater equanimity and with less trauma to one's self. People's faults, limits, and assets are seen with greater clarity, as part of the whole of the person, and are therefore viewed with more reality and compassion. There is increased satisfaction and appreciation of the stuff of everyday life: food, water, air, sunlight, faces, children, flowers, various events.

The world is less idealized and there are fewer crashes and disappointments with it. Events of all kinds are seen and felt as part of a large framework and experienced with greater equanimity.

If "laid back" doesn't mean "held back," what does it mean?

It means being at peace with one's self, or being relatively relaxed. It means that top priority is given to having a valid sense of one's self rather than feeling amorphously caught up and lost in any kind of frenetic activity or "rat race."

This is not detachment! Detachment is an obsessive fear and entails a compulsive need to avoid involvement. Laid back means having enough integrity and autonomy to be able to choose freely the areas and people in which and with whom involvement is desirable. Real involvement is possible only with a real self. The laid-back self has not been ground down and diluted by any aspect of the culture. The laid-back self is real.

In this philosophy what is the most important human prerogative?

The most important human prerogative derives from the fact that we are now instinct-free. This enables us to choose what we do, how we do it, and the rate at which we do it. In other words, our most important prerogative is having a choice of how we use the time of our lives.

Is there one sure sign of increased mellowness?

Feeling peacefully better without the use of drugs, stimulating events, reassurance, victories, or accomplishments of any kind constitute evidence of mellow growth.

Are you against accomplishment?

I am against *compulsive* accomplishment at the expense of one's self. Accomplishment that comes of self-enhancing activity is fine but its importance is secondary to the activity itself. In other words, I see the most serious accomplishment as personal change and growth. The second most serious accomplishment is aiding another person's change and growth.

Are competitive sports antithetical to being mellow?

This depends on the players. If the players are relatively mellow and if playing is more important than winning and if the people involved on both sides are always held in higher regard than the game and the goal, relative mellowness may be sustained.

Does being "mellow" and lacking in aggression result in poor athletic performance? Don't nice guys finish last?

Being mellow may make for less vindictive, ruthless antagonists. If they are mellow, athletes, like participants in any of life's activities, are able to make maximum use of good reflexes and smooth movement. This is probably what "being cool" is all about. Of course pleasure in the activity itself must replace stimulation gleaned from vindictive triumph.

Being mellow means that satisfaction is largely derived from a feeling of physical self-realization rather than from putting down an adversary. Mellow participants are less likely to suffer from the vicissitudes of a manic-depressive society. Mellow, relaxed athletes are also less subject to injury than uptight, ruthless, glory-seeking athletes.

Can a part of one's self that has been troublesome and has exacted too great a price eventually be eradicated?

For example, let us take a man who has always valued freedom from sustained involvement but has always wanted the benefits of a permanent loving relationship. He finally has the possibility of a wonderful relationship but feels depressed because if he commits himself and gets married, his freedom will be gone. If he sustains his freedom he will lose the girl. In either case he feels a sense of depressing loss. If he does commit himself and marries, will he eventually be able to eradicate his need for freedom, especially since he knows the freedom has never brought him any great rewards?

No part of one's self is ever eradicated! It is never possible to satisfy all parts of one's self at the same time! A price must be paid; something must give; something always must be relinquished. Some aspects of self must be frustrated. In this case, freedom from involvement will suffer when commitment through marriage takes place. The yearning for freedom will continue. However, the strength of its effect will depend on the degree of reconciliation with it. I know one man who cannot reconcile himself to loss of freedom and becomes severely alcoholic each time he forms a serious relationship. This is his attempt to obliterate the conflict. It doesn't work. Repression doesn't work. Nothing works perfectly. People are complex and many aspects of themselves will never be satisfied. To the extent that they can be conscious of all aspects of themselves, of the price they choose to pay relative to their priorities, they will live lives of relative reconciliation and relative inner peace.

What are cultural or societal timetables?

These are conventional beliefs or ideas about chronological age, and what positions, attainments, activities, and commencements are appropriate or inappropriate relative to age. Thus, we should be finished with college by such and such age, should be married by a given age and retired by a certain age; it's too late to start medical school after a certain age; and so forth. These timetables exist, both consciously and unconsciously, and exert an extremely powerful influence in our lives. They are insidious and ruthless and have little regard for individual differences, needs, talents, or proclivities. They are offshoots of the same psychology that lies behind other prejudices and behind stereotyped, rigid, constricted thinking. They must be vigorously guarded against when we make decisions in our lives because they serve the purpose of inertia, resignation, and hopelessness, thus feeding self-corrosion and inner turmoil.

How important is humor in aiding inner peace?

Humor dilutes common pressures of everyday life—it defuses solemnity and restores a sense of appropriate balance.

Does being open to advice come under the heading of being open to goodness?

Yes, good advice is goodness and the wisdom and experience of others can be valuable. Of course this applies only if we retain our own judgment and make our own decisions. Slavish compliance with any advice, however good, is a form of self-rejection and is as destructive as compulsive rebellious closure to advice.

Does power corrupt people?

I believe that corrupt, sick, driven people inevitably make corrupt and perverse use of power. I feel that healthy, benevolent people can use power for the common good. Of course, knowing the difference can be very difficult and I believe, like so many other people, that it is therefore safest to dilute power through democratic distribution.

Are there any particular situations in which it is of practical and vital importance to surrender or to capitulate?

Sickness and treatment are important ones, and surrender to limitations incurred by the former and being open to the latter can be lifesaving. Treatment imposed on reluctant and resistant patients is always hampered and is often ineffectual. This is particularly true in sicknesses that involve stress, such as heart attacks and psychosomatic manifestations like bronchial asthma, dermatological manifestations, and gastrointestinal disturbances.

We should also surrender in situations in which we are truly helpless—not going into burning buildings that are about to collapse, not continuing in businesses that have long been doomed to failure, and not pursuing hopeless, unrequited love affairs.

Of course we do well to surrender to practical reality in situations that involve impossible attempts to surpass individual limitations, physical, intellectual, emotional, or any other.

In this outlook does "cultural success" play any role?

Satisfaction in what we commonly think of as cultural achievement and satisfaction in terms of self-realization are not necessarily mutually exclusive. But on the other hand, self-realizing efforts may be sacrificed to efforts made for cultural success goals, and this is antithetical to inner peace. I do not suggest that it is easy to ignore cultural goals and at the same time to sustain self-esteem. For example, it is difficult to ignore the accumulation of money as a goal in a money-oriented society. But if money takes primacy over more important aspects of living, and if it is used not for real needs but for ostentatious desires, inner peace will be obliterated.

Does sexual activity or lack of it play a significant role in reconciliation and inner peace?

I do not believe that sexual activity plays any role in health directly but its indirect role can be great. I believe that sex reflects our relating activity generally and that poor satisfaction in sexual relations is often a reflection of poor relating on every level. I feel that sexual frustration and difficulties, plus poor satisfaction in relating generally, creates enough stress to be destructive to relative inner peace, equilibrium, happiness, and health.

If we are free of instinctual drives, why do infants suck for milk almost as soon as they are born?

I think that reflex reactions—feeling a sugar depletion or empty stomach leading to reflex sucking—must be differentiated from instinct-dictated behavior. Instinct-driven creatures are "told" what to do in almost all areas of their lives. I feel that even if we regard ourselves as instinct-directed at birth, we leave these residual directives behind once we become fully developed adults. Perhaps this is a case of ontology recapitulating ontogeny—or the growth of the organism mimicking the development of the species.

Isn't man the only species who kills his own kind without purpose, and doesn't this demonstrate inborn or instinctual aggression?

I believe that members of other species attack and kill each other under adverse circumstances, such as undue stress caused by unusual crowding. I believe that aggression is not an inborn or instinctual characteristic in people but rather a learned response and evidence of inner as well as cultural aberration.

What can I do if I feel an "attack of vindictiveness" coming on?

Leave the scene, person, or event that is felt as the stimulating source and the potential recipient of the oncoming attack and walk it off. Then sit down and try to reason out which pride-invested area in yourself was hurt or threatened and must be surrendered.

But what do I do if someone with a different philosophy attacks me?

You defend yourself, and if the only possible defense includes attack or "fighting back," you do that. But if you must attack there is a vast difference between doing it with regret and doing it with glee and joy of vindictive triumph. Of course any kind of prophylaxis or communicative struggle for the purpose of promoting peace is best done during peace and not war.

Do people who become professional soldiers suffer from undue need for aggressive expression or vindictive triumph?

I think that many of them are basically morbid, dependent people who have a strong need to be told what to do. They are afraid of choice and of making decisions. Some are afraid of disorder and insecurity or what they may feel as too much freedom. Many people like this repress a great deal of anger, which may be rationalized as patriotic fervor and displaced and expressed through acceptable aggressive acts as a means of quelling anxiety.

Are anxiety and anger related?

I feel that threatened or incipient emergence of repressed anger in people who have a compulsive need to be liked (especially true of morbid, dependent, self-effacing, compliant, conforming people) is translated into anxiety. This I feel is the biggest cause or producer of anxiety. The biggest cause of strong anger is hurt pride.

Why does it so often take a heart attack or some other horrendous sickness or event to get someone off the glory road and out of the rat race?

Many of us don't consciously know that we are on a glory road or that we are jeopardizing our lives. Some of us know but feel that we are omnipotent and can get away with it. The heart attack provides evidence to the contrary, and for the moment in effect initiates a kind of dialogue.

What happens is this. The true self says to the idealized, glory-seeking self, "You better leave me alone, let me rest, let me relax and just be; otherwise this heart attack will kill us both and you never will get what you want." The idealized self says, "Okay, no pressure, no shoulds, no expectations to be filled—for now, but when you are back on your feet I'll be back." Depending on the emotional health of the person in question he will or will not get "back into harness." But he will surely hear from all glory-seeking aspects of himself again. Of course those people who can embark upon the struggle to get out of the rat race without paying the price of a life-threatening event are much better candidates for continued mellow living. This is so because their motivation comes from well-grounded insight rather than imposed threat to life.

What makes people duplicitous?

The biggest cause of duplicity is the need to be liked. It is not some inborn hypocrisy or malevolent, Machiavellian streak of selfishness or ruthlessness. Self-effacement and the need to be liked stand in the way of being oneself and telling it the way it is. The self-effacing, compliant person's desperate need to be universally loved precludes honesty; he or she cannot take the risk of spontaneous, honest expression, which might incur another person's disfavor. Such people sometimes seem gossipy and even malicious because they will cater to adversaries in an effort to curry favor with both. Quite often, too, they will convince themselves of beliefs they would not otherwise have, in an effort to subvert their own feelings in order to please other people. The tragedy here is multifold. Relationships are disturbed; spontaneous self is lost; uptight, constricted, studied behavior replaces easygoing, unstressful, mellow moods and feelings.

Are there places and activities that are antithetical to mellow living, or is it just a question of our own individual psychologies and an overall stress-producing culture? Why don't people change situations more readily?

Of course all factors contribute and we cannot play down the role of individual psychodynamics. But there certainly are places and occupations or subcultures that are more stress-producing than others. There are many situations that are particularly inimical to ordinary human needs, especially those involving time—time for leisure, time for self, and the time it takes to do various tasks.

But the worst places, occupations, or situations of any kind in terms of personal stress are those that, deep down, we don't want, those that are incompatible with real tastes, proclivities, pace, and rhythms. Many people feel caught in particular situations because of convention or because of "security needs" or because of money. Many are caught because they feel they cannot leave a situation in which they are "successful," even though they are miserable where they are. This is particularly true of "successful" businessmen whose only real success is in making more and more money, which they often can enjoy less and less. Many people can't or won't leave because of fear of unfamiliar situations. Some are unaware of the enormous capacity of human beings to make new adaptations, especially those that basically are intensely desired and compatible with one's well-being.

Many people cannot leave because they make an unconscious contract with themselves excluding the possibility of returning, or of changing situations repeatedly until one is found consistent with needs or desires. Fear of "embarrassment" and potential self-recriminations often cause inhibition, paralysis, and even complete lack of awareness that options exist. Fear of "failure" can be so great as to obliterate any awareness that dissatisfaction with current conditions exists at all. I have seen many people over the years who were very unhappy without any awareness at all that the status quo was in any way responsible for their misery. This of course is no surprise in a culture that abounds with self-delusion and duplicity.

I particularly remember one man who, after much struggle, finally decided on a change of occupation and location. Unfortunately when I asked him what he would do if he didn't like the change, he replied, "I'll like it even if I don't like it."

Is "taking one's self seriously" compatible with being fun-loving?

Absolutely! The culture often confuses us into believing that seriousness consists of solemnity, heaviness, and pretense. Nothing can be farther from the truth. Seriousness is made up of authenticity and devotion to self-realization. Taking one's self seriously involves knowledge of self, care of self, and nourishment of self. Loving fun, not to be confused with addiction to stimulation and highs, is certainly an important ingredient of taking one's self seriously. Of course fun is different for different people relative to individual tastes and proclivities.

You have said that boredom is a failure to make adequate use of one's own resources and is antithetical to inner peace and well-being. But isn't it possible to be bored from the outside, by certain people?

If there are people in whom we cannot find interest we must ask ourselves how come we cannot use our inner resources to sustain any interest in them. The answer may be that they offer us little authenticity or substance of real self. It may also be that their resistance to change and growth is so great that they are in a state of paralysis. If this is the case we must then ask ourselves if we can or want to overcome our boredom by helping them overcome their pretense and/or paralysis, or do we prefer to sever our relationships with them. To continue in a state of boredom gives them nothing and is antithetical to our own well-being, since boredom contributes to further neglect of our inner resources.

Why must people answer the phone when it rings even if the working day is over and if they are "taking it easy" and don't feel like talking?

Addiction to responsibility or to stimulation or to both is usually the reason. Loyalty to self and to care of self helps to dilute the grandiose need to be "always there" for other people. Not answering the phone can eventually dilute the need for "stimulating news" or constant contact with others. But this means taking a stand against a cultural dictum. The fact is that the imperious ring of the telephone has for most of us taken precedence over conversation with anyone who is physically in our presence. "Getting through" to some people is for that reason easier by phone than it is in person.

Is it best to set aside time each day for taking it easy or napping, as well as vacation time several times a year—all of which would be inviolate?

As an emergency measure and if this is what is for the moment possible, scheduling time to relax can be constructive. However, this amounts to scheduling oneself to be unscheduled. In this way the process itself, while turned to constructive use, indicates the need to go a bit farther.

The idea is to not permit oneself to be so inundated with "responsibility" and achievement-oriented activity as to lose touch with one's rhythms and needs. We need to know when we need a rest, when we want to relax, when we want a change of place or a change of rhythm—"just to lie around." If our lives offer us sufficient choice so that we are able to satisfy these needs spontaneously in our society, we are fortunate indeed. But even if we can't "take off" whenever we want to—and there are many of us who can but don't—we are much better off if we are at least tuned in to what we need and want without requiring schedules to tell us.

Doesn't everyone require about the same amount of sleep?

Absolutely not! Variation in this area is enormous, varying from people who require as little as a few hours of sleep a night to those who need twelve or more hours a night. Some people get along with only a few short catnaps during the day. But many people have come to believe that they must have at least eight hours of sleep a night. Some of them toss and turn all night in an effort to comply with this dictum. As a result some people become terribly fatigued attempting to sleep, and take this as further proof of the compelling need for "at least eight hours of sleep.'' In an effort to comply and to be allowed to feel good, some become habituated to sleeping pills.

The real point is that many people, inundated by cultural pressures, have lost touch with their own rhythms and needs. Reestablishing contact with one's own needs and going along with them can be difficult but can also be constructively life-changing and even lifesaving. Everyone does not require the same food; is not attracted to the same people; does not walk, talk, eat the same way or at the same rate; does not like the same house to live in or the same clothes to wear; does not have the same sexual needs or appetites or rhythms, and on and on it goes—despite cultural bombardment that would flatten us out into compliant, conforming, universally acceptable units.

Isn't a certain amount of pretense sometimes necessary in our society—for example, when a salesman pretends enthusiasm in order to sell a product?

Unfortunately, duplicity and pretense are sometimes necessary in order to save our lives, and I'm all for saving our lives. Acting as if we are not who we are can be necessary in the face of an enemy who wants nothing less than our death.

But—and this is a big but—it is important for us to be fully aware that we are pretending when we do so and to stop pretending when the need no longer exists.

Too many of us pretend and do not know it. We are caught in an intricate web of pretense and cannot extricate ourselves because we no longer can discern pretense from real self.

What, then, is the antithesis of pretense from a practical point of view?

Any activity on behalf of change and growth works against pretense.

For me, reconciliation of the various aspects of self is

the core device in destroying pretense. It must be remembered that pretense is studied, wooden, mechanical, and deadening. In pretense, aspects of self that are not in keeping with the picture one is attempting to convey are repressed and diverted from the mainstream.

Reconciliation works in the opposite direction. It integrates and invites all aspects of self to unite for alive spontaneity, full consciousness (without self-consciousness), and full self-acceptance as part of the self-loving mainstream.

How is self-love different from narcissism?

Self-love involves nourishment of real self, promoting change and growth. Narcissism is born of self-hate; the victim compulsively seeks nourishment of the pretended self in any of its manifestations.

Self-love involves the generation of love or caring for other people too. Narcissism excludes caring about other people for fear of self-depletion.

How about "real time," or time as the clock measures it?

Clock time measures the rate at which the clock hands move and the earth rotates on its axis and moves around the sun. While this is very useful for us to apply to schedules and appointments, the most important and *real* time for us is psychological time or how we perceive change in terms of rate and quality.

What is the effect on friendships of dropping affectations and becoming a "more real person"?

Some relationships are terminated. When the "role" in set scenarios is dropped, the other players sometimes get confused, angry, and anxious and drop the relationship. Other relationships become open, real, and constructive for the first time as other participants become inspired to drop pretenses also.

Changes in status quo are particularly difficult in

closely relating groups, especially in families. A reshuffling of positions is invariably necessary at some point, and this is usually traumatic to the people who have the most to lose in terms of their positions of pretense and rigidity.

Some groups can tolerate reverberations and can even become healthier as a result. Others break apart. Some exert great pressure in the hope that the individual who has struggled through to newfound self and honesty may be forced back into role-playing, rather than quitting the group altogether.

How do you feel about the expression, "so-and-so has arrived"?

The expression is a fraud. The implication and implicit promise is that there is a status that is achievable called "having arrived." The further implication is that "once having arrived," the person is safe, impervious to most of life's insults and assaults, and will live happily ever after. Of course all of this is the stuff of cultural mythology.

In terms of change and growth one never "arrives" but rather keeps growing, and of course there is no position of guaranteed safety or predictability in life.

In terms of delusional self-glorification one never arrives but remains ever driven in search of new conquests, more narcissistic supplies, and more glory.

Is it possible to feel more or less peaceful or anxious in the presence of different people?

Yes! As I explained in the second section, there are relationships that are best terminated. But there are relationships, especially with relatives, that are very difficult to break. Some of these are best diluted by the presence of other people when visits cannot be avoided. The fact is that none of us are immune from old memories and unpleasant associations, which some people bring up in us. Coping with these on a conscious level

helps; nonetheless, people and situations will always exist who threaten our equanimity. Of course intrapsychic
change and greater reconciliation help us withstand all
kinds of outside onslaughts or negative effects, but they
do not preclude anxiety in difficult situations.

*Do "uptight" people know that they are anxious and
stressed?*

A few do and many do not. But nearly all of them
know that "something is missing," that, no matter how
calm and collected they appear to others, they feel
"knotted up" inside, or "feel like exploding."

*In keeping with the concept of respect for individual
rhythms, aren't there some people who move more
quickly than others, are quicker and bouncier and more
energetic? Isn't asking them to slow down and to
mellow imposing another kind of dictum on them?*

If people are comfortable and compatible with fast
pacing there is no reason to ask them to slow down.
They can be mellow only if they retain rhythms that
are uniquely their own. In our society, however, most
people in most activities are asked to speed up regardless
of how fast they are already moving. They are asked to
surrender individual rhythms in favor of required schedules and are judged accordingly. Thus, as I indicated in
answer to an earlier question, there are timetables for
when to eat (whether or not we are hungry); when to ur-
inate and have bowel movements (regardless of natural
urges); at what age to be finished with one school level
and ready for another; at what age to walk and to talk;
rate at which sexual excitation and need ought to occur;
at what age to become a company vice president or chief
of a hospital service, and so forth.

Of course it is beneficial to go along with one's own
unique rhythms and not to apply a blanket slowdown or
speedup. Trouble arises because many people are oblivious to the pace and rhythms they are comfortable with,

having early on surrendered to all kinds of cultural scheduling and pacing.

One artist I treated was not painting well, though he had done excellent work in the past. It turned out that he had complied with the suggestions of other people and had radically changed his work routine several years before coming to see me. He had in the past always worked in spurts—painting intensely for hours at a time, then resting for prolonged periods, and then painting again when he got the urge. For the last several years he had "disciplined" himself and painted several hours a day on schedule. He admitted that the urge was gone. At my suggestion he stopped painting altogether until his urge to paint returned. It did and he went back to his own earlier pattern, satisfying his own "creative clock." His painting improved radically and the anxiety and depression that brought him to me in the first place became considerably reduced. Of course we still had to work on his compelling need to comply and to conform and the ease with which he was willing to ignore his own serious needs. During the course of treatment it became evident that this self-effacing trend existed in almost all areas of his life. Pleasing others and getting approval from others had almost done away with loyalty to himself, which had to be re-established.

At what age do we start ignoring our own needs and rhythms?

Usually very early in life and as a response to fear. The very young child whose self-esteem has been hurt because he feels that he lives in an essentially hostile environment starts abandoning himself in favor of "safety." This "safety" often takes the form of establishing an image and a set of rules that he feels will be safer than being his own self. One aspect of the image largely entails grandiose mastery, another comprises freedom from involvement, and still another consists of self-effacement and compliance. Most of us suffer from an amalgam of all three and as a result are in chronic unconscious internal conflict as "shoulds" and "should nots" make conflicting demands on us. As the years go by this image becomes solidified and complicated, eventually permeating all aspects of the personality. Further solidification and complication takes place as a result of cultural pressure, which is largely derived through parents early in life and then continues as a direct force when one "gets out into the world."

Is there any single thing that can be done to reestablish one's natural rhythm?

Time off for reevaluation of how we feel about ourselves relative to how we spend the time of our lives is helpful. This means really taking time off from all activity and sitting quietly with ourselves so as to get reacquainted with who we are. This ought to be done every once in a while and must be viewed as a most serious act. Of course it can only be done and only has meaning if we are sufficiently loyal to ourselves so that our top priority is our own well-being.

Isn't there a kind of noninvolved detachment which takes place in mellow living?

No! Detachment, undue priority given to freedom from involvement, is compulsive and is an attempt to mitigate anxiety and fear of inundation by people. It comes from a sense of fragility, vulnerability, and is used as an attempt to avoid and to escape both inner and external conflict.

Mellow living is a function of real self and real choice. The detached person seems to have unusual integrity because of nondilution by other people. The mellow person sustains integrity even as intercourse with other people takes place. The mellow person is not vulnerable to inundation and dilution by others because the self is well-integrated and identity is solidly established and felt. The give and take with other people, missing in the lives of detached people, is enriching to mellow people. Indeed, one of the great benefits of being mellow is caring about other people, as well as being open to goodness, which largely comes from other people. These aspects are relatively muted in detached people. Mellow people retain choice and retain their own value systems despite outside pressures. This retention of self may be seen as detachment but is no such thing. It is simply the antithesis of compulsive conformity.

Can openness to goodness supersede psychoanalytic treatment?

I believe that people who are very closed often need analytic treatment to become open. It is the work of psychoanalysis to open people up to themselves. We do this by making conscious and available many of the feelings that were repressed and relegated to unconsciousness. In the process of treatment, cynicism, bitterness, and closure are diluted so that greater openness to goodness becomes possible. If the course of treatment does not increase openness to goodness I consider the treatment to be of very limited value.

Where relative openness to goodness exists, psychoanalysis may be valuable but is seldom necessary. If a person can struggle and become open to goodness, I feel that the possibility of amelioration of self on all levels may be so significant as to preclude the necessity of treatment.

How does fatigue fit into this philosophical framework?

Being relatively reconciled has the effect of diminishing fatigue. Fatigue that is the result of unreconciled conflict, of strained behavior and working against the real self should be considerably diminished. But there is also increased respect for fatigue, meaning that when we are tired we do not fight it. We are not insulted by it. We don't ignore it. We enjoy it as an utterly human condition and we enjoy it by ample resting, vacationing, sleeping, and "doing nothing."

Is it possible to "do nothing?"

It is possible to do nothing that is relatively goal-directed or accomplishment-oriented.

In a broad and deep sense we cannot "do nothing." Our hearts, our digestive systems are always doing something. When we walk or talk we are doing something. We are living continuums and our lives go on without any hiatus or even periods of hibernation. The closest we come to "doing nothing" is sleep, and it is becoming increasingly evident to most of us that sleep is actually a very active time in our lives.

Therefore, by "doing nothing" I mean *nothing* in the way of goal-directed work. I mean slowing down enough to have a sense of ourselves. I have learned to sit around virtually empty-headed for an hour or more at a time, and I find this to be replenishing and relieving of fatigue, which usually seems to be fatigue from doing things. Of course during these "do nothing" periods I'm really doing a number of things such as breathing, feeling, seeing, hearing. I suspect that "doing nothing" is a highly individual matter and that each of us has a unique way of doing it. Many of us, however, do not practice the process of "doing nothing" enough and are not responsive enough to fatigue. Some of us have even become oblivious to feeling tired and do not know how tired we've become until we are severely exhausted or until dire psychological and physical repercussions occur.

What is the role of kindness in the reconciled, mellow framework?

Kindness is not forced. I feel that being kind is a natural human proclivity and is the very basis of co-operative relating. Mutual openness and caring are the stuff of kindness. Being kind is therapeutic to all concerned, and particularly so to those of us who can be kind to ourselves as well as to others. Indeed one invariably follows the other. Kindness cannot be feigned or manufactured in the service of a glory-seeking Christ-like image. In the absence of real caring and real acceptance of other people's rhythms, needs, and differences, what looks like kindness is self-serving, contrived, and patronizing. This kind of "facsimile"—subtly and sometimes without the consciousness of the "donor"—satisfies hidden needs for competition and "soft" vindictive triumphs.

Is there a discernible difference between true creative work of the authentic self and work that is produced skillfully but solely in order to impress or for other secondary gain?

Authentic expression nearly always has at least some therapeutic effect. The effect can best be described as mending and binding. It mends inner hurts, binds the self together, and makes the further expression of authentic feelings possible. Authentic production may entail considerable struggle but a unique and deep satisfaction often accompanies the process.

If becoming "great" or struggling for "greatness" is a form of competition and even aggression, is there anything potentially great in human beings? Were men such as Freud and Einstein great?

Yes. I am wary of the term *great* because I feel that considerable damage is done in the quest for "greatness" and the worship of "greatness" by individuals, groups, and nations. I feel that some people have greater skills than others. I agree that some people have very rare or unique talents. I believe that many people have the ability to struggle through to greater cooperative living and to greater compassion for themselves and the human condition generally. Perhaps, considering their extraordinary position of being instinct-free, members of our species are at their "greatest" when they succeed at all in their struggle for humility. In this regard nearly all members of the species have a capacity for "greatness."

Are kindness and cooperative relating and the therapeutic effects of helping others possible only for the very healthy among us?

It is difficult to help others and to live cooperatively in a state of great self-doubt and fear of self-depletion, and with strong feelings of self-hate projected onto others and converted into paranoid states in which others become the enemy. It is difficult to perceive other people's needs in states of overwhelming narcissism. However, I believe that even when we are at our sickest, even at the height of narcissistic preoccupation, we are still capable of at least some genuine kindness. Of course, as with all other areas of human activity, this is relative, and the healthier we are, the more the self-realizing process is fulfilled, the greater our capacity for cooperation and kindness.

If we take time with relationships, waiting to get to know each other really well, will this lead to our liking each other more?

According to recent studies by reliable sociologists, the more we know each other, the more we like each other. This may be due to several facts. Long-term relationships are long-term because they have, so to speak, been put to the test. People who don't like each other break up before relationships become long-term. Also, getting to know each other allays suspicions and threats. Additionally, time is permitted to invest feelings and to develop caring as well as to become familiar with new ideas and common interests. For some time I have felt that interest follows involvement. We need to become involved in order to see if we are interested.

Of course some people get to dislike each other, but for all kinds of secondary reasons (such as the sick satisfactions of sadomasochistic relationships) sustain the relationship. However, taking time to evolve relationships slowly gives us an opportunity to profit from good relationships that might otherwise have been aborted, and serves to prevent the pain of overinvestment in people we have not had ample time to get to know.

What are some of the basic ingredients of kindness?

Basic ingredients of kindness include— appreciation for each other's limits, problems, fallibilities, rhythms, needs, proclivities, vulnerabilities, and sensitivities; listening to each other speak; not withholding openness of expression from each other; giving each other ample time and room to be separate and alone; giving help when needed.

Why do we seem to shun change as we get older? Is it because we have gotten too used to certain ways?

I believe that this is a culturally induced self-fulfilling prophecy. Older people are really in an ideal position to make changes, because they have more experiences to tap and to use in the service of desired changes. When people can't or won't change it is not a question of being too used to old ways as much as a question of resignation. Unfortunately, our society helps to push older people into a state of paralyzing chronic resignation by depriving them of the right to participate fully in life's offerings.

How can we evaluate our lives if not in terms of having been either successes or failures?

The best alternative is no judgmental evaluation along these lines at all. These are almost always either self-condemning or self-glorifying expeditions having little to do with humanity or reality. The only "evaluation" I deem worthwhile is more accurately called an *exploration*. I speak here of a periodic nonmoralizing, nonjudgmental, nonequivocating exploration or constructive perception, to be done during life and not as an end-of-life pass/fail review. Its purpose is a dynamic one: to discover further areas for potential increase in self-realization.

Does the mellow or reconciled philosophy have any principal tenet regarding living together?

If there is one I would say it is "Live and let live." This really means no inundation by one member of another; no exploitation; no melding into a two-headed eight-limbed monster. It means living as two distinctly separate human whole selves who make all kinds of open exchanges while they sustain their individuality.

Doesn't it help us work more smoothly, with less anxiety and pressure, if we first sit down, think things through, and make necessary decisions and plans?

Some issues and actions require thinking, decisions, and planning. Many do not! Very often "thinking and deciding" are useless ruminations used to avoid doing. There are a great many things that are better done, done more easily and naturally, spontaneously, freshly, and usefully by simply doing them with our whole beings and with no verbalization at all.

I know a sculptor who works this way. His works are expressed through his hands, which represent his whole being when they work on clay. For these works he neither decides nor plans; he just does the work, his hands using the clay to express his feelings.

The best way to break through all kinds of blocks is simply to do and not to think. This applies to writing, too. Sometimes a writer is blocked for a number of reasons: perfectionistic needs; temporary loss of self-esteem and self-confidence; repressed anger; or preoccupation with other problem areas of his or her life. It is often useful simply to write whatever comes to mind relative to the subject, with total disregard of plan, goal, or logic. Interestingly, these free associations, free of decision-making or conscious, logical processes, often turn out to have connections, which eventually manifest themselves and so the block is broken. Worrying and pushing and thinking and attempting to force with deciding and planning often make for still more inhibition and paralysis.

Do prestige-seeking people in our culture ever reach a level where they are finally satisfied and no longer have to push on ad infinitum? There are people who do become presidents and some who do get the Nobel Prize.

If prestige is secondary to one's sense of self-realization, it is appreciated and it is enough. If prestige comes as a result of seeking prestige as a primary goal, it is never enough. Indeed, for these people each new plateau reached or peak climbed whets the appetite for still more.

This is so because the goal—prestige or power or money—in no way solves or mitigates the underlying difficulty or problem. The individual who suffers from inner fragmentation and lack of self-esteem uses the culture to develop the illusion that prestige will mend him. It does not, and with each achievement, the solace he may feel becomes more fleeting. Unfortunately, his interpretation of the results does not lead him to get to the heart of the problem but rather to seek still more prestige; eventually he becomes addicted to prestige and loath to surrender it, lest he have to confront the truth.

Many middle-aged people ask the question, "Am I doing meaningful things in the time I have left in my life?" Is this a constructive question or exercise?

I think most questions involving "time left" are destructive pressure-makers. Such questions may look good, but I believe that they reflect the ulterior motive of trying to build a self-glorifying monument, and that they are actually not designed to promote self-realization. It can be valuable "to look in on ourselves" and to see if we are happy with what we are doing. But this seldom involves concern with being "meaningful" or with "time left," nor is this reserved for middle age or any other.

Can insatiable appetites of all kinds be curtailed or diluted?

Yes, but only by understanding that they are invariably symbolic of deeper needs that must be uncovered and dealt with on a realistic basis. For example, I know a woman who could not give up an insatiable need for suffering and depression, years after she lost her husband through divorce. She was finally able to do so when she realized that she had come to believe that to stop suffering was to surrender the possibility of his coming back, while to continue to suffer would sustain and even actualize that possibility. Other people eat insatiably to fill voids in their lives that have nothing at all to do with food. Still others, suffering from unconscious feelings of inadequacy, take risks of all kinds to test themselves against confused criteria of masculinity.

Can a person's tolerance for frustration, pain, and anxiety be increased?

A mellow attitude and philosophical outlook mitigates any exigency that comes up as part of the human condition. The snowball effect of becoming anxious about being anxious is lessened, and the same is true of pain and frustration. There is less hurt pride about "How can this happen to me?" and less hurt pride about being helpless, and this also mitigates pain and frustration.

Any lessening of tension, any increase in relaxation has the effect of increasing stress tolerance generally. Of course an increase in the ability to wait, to be in harmony with whatever is happening at the moment, "to ride with it," cushions and comforts at times of disequilibrium.

Of course the entire frame of reference of reconciliation makes for less frustration, anxiety, and even pain because expectations are markedly reduced and human activity on all levels is perceived and experienced with increased reality.

Some people are in particular torment when they must wait for the return of a loved one. Is their pain directly proportional to the intensity of their love?

This kind of pain is almost always the result of morbid dependency. The individual suffers from a need to merge with another self in order to feel whole. When separated from the other person he or she feels torn apart and without a self—thus the anxiety and pain. Learning to wait helps dilute this kind of morbid dependency, and any dilution of morbid dependency makes waiting more tolerable, thus contributing to a constructive cycle.

How can we avoid being pushed by time in the complicated worlds in which most of us live?

Many of us are overscheduled. Our working lives are segmented by long-standing prearranged routines. We must periodically engage in a process I call *unscheduling,* in which we review our schedules and do what we can to recoup as much free time for ourselves as possible.

Many of us unfortunately also inflict heavy schedules on our children, who from a very early age are shipped from one activity to another and hardly ever have the experience of being free of schedules.

From my point of view, this obsession with scheduling is a form of alienation from feelings and a running from the freedom to use time spontaneously, as we will.

The schedule takes the place of feelings, moods, desires, choices, decisions, and free actions.

In this connection I also advise caution about commitments involving stringent deadlines. Some of us become trapped by a "malignancy of deadlines" and this exerts even more pressure and stress than scheduling. As I indicated in Part II, using deadlines or compulsory due dates as motivation to get things done is a form of self-hate and cruelty to self, the very antithesis of the mellow philosophy.

Also, it is my feeling that most people function best when they are not harassed and not coerced. If they cannot function without overscheduling and malignant deadlining, it is only because they have become slave to this kind of time-robbing; they must do their best to extricate themselves so as to reinitiate freedom and spontaneity. One of the arguments we hear for scheduling and speeding things up is: "There's hardly any time left." We must counter that with: "There is plenty of time left"—there almost always is for things that are really meaningful to us.

If there are no "instant relationships," what about the chemistry that takes place between some people instantly on meeting, even before words are spoken?

We do relate instantly and relationships begin the instant any contact at all takes place. Actually, many relationships are already set in motion before people have met or talked. Being told about each other by a third person starts relating feelings going. Rubbing shoulders begins the relating process. We relate to whomever we even slightly notice, even when contact is minimal and shortlived (an instant) and never renewed.

Every contact stirs some feeling, memory, thought, association, however subtle and however unconscious. The "across a crowded room" chemistry is often part of relating to the "projected ideal" that each of us carries in mind.

But this instant relating is not to be confused with a long-standing relationship, which, like a long book, is not written until it is written, is not there until considerable relating and knowing each other has taken place. *Instant big emotional investments* in instant-relating partners often bring long-standing emotional headaches.

How do vindictive triumph and the drive to create envy really work? Why are they destructive to the individual using them?

Their purpose is to feed pride and to bolster up hurt pride. Pride and real self are not on the same wavelength. Feeding pride or restoring hurt pride may result in "feeling good" from temporary self-inflation but it does not add to increased self-esteem and sets the individual up for another fall. Additionally, the desire to create envy in others is directly proportional to the pain we feel when others create envy in us, or whenever we feel envy, for whatever reason.

What happens to relationships when formerly self-effacing people become straightforward, drop their duplicity, and no longer "play the game" or "take part in the play"?

Much depends on how much the other participants help, as well as the degree of real involvement or healthy exchange. If the participants are very duplicitous themselves, and if the relationship has been founded mainly on neurotic needs, the relationship will usually break up. If the participants are relatively healthy and if some of the stuff of real selves has been exchanged, the relationships will improve and there will be an increase in the honest exchange of feelings and ideas.

Can reconciliation be described very simply as "coming to terms with"?

Yes, coming to terms with all aspects of ourselves

even as we negotiate the society in which we live may be considered an overall way of putting it.

What is the single most common cause of psychological pain?

Psychological pain is due to self-flagellation, often unconscious, following hurt pride as a result of a fall from one's exalted self-image. The best healer is compassion for one's self. The best prophylactic agent is humility. Fear of the consequences of "failure" makes for inhibition and inability to function and especially to try new things with relative ease and comfort.

How do we know when people are being compassionate with us as differentiated from patronizing us?

We know largely by the results: how we respond to them, how we feel in their presence. If they are compassionate with us we feel good. If they patronize us we feel demeaned and angry. The key ingredient is respect. When we have compassion for people we respect them and their individual needs. There is no "talking down" to exploit them surreptitiously and promote our own superiority. Patronizing people involves contempt for them and an attempt to manipulate them for selfish purposes. If we cannot tolerate compassion and kindness directed at ourselves we must look inside ourselves for problems of considerable sick pride covering chronic and deep self-hate.

The inability to receive kindness from others is a serious deterrent to constructive relating and produces chronic stress.

If we have difficulty with and anxiety in relationships with other people, should we consider living alone as a means to inner peace?

Living in virtual isolation as an attempt to cope with this kind of problem does not work.

Seclusive and reclusive behavior usually results in

constriction and is an impediment to the free flow of feelings necessary to a state of relative comfort and equilibrium. I believe that nearly all recluses are intensely angry people who cannot deal with their feelings on a level appropriate to their own needs and well-being. People who live in isolation do so compulsively, not out of choice, but usually out of great fear of other people and society, as well as deep feelings of personal inadequacy and cynicism and bitterness.

Many people live this kind of life as a way of saying "I don't need anyone at all" and thus sustaining hurt pride.

Does intellect play a significant role in the struggle for self-realization and inner peace?

It helps to be able to conceptualize the principles involved, but I feel that self-realization is a question more of motivation than of intellect. People of both lesser and greater intellectual endowment seem capable of both inner turmoil and relative equanimity.

Does it help to emulate someone who seems to have achieved inner peace?

To imitate is just that and nothing more. Some people are good actors and "emulate" on the surface while they seethe inwardly and sometimes even become explosive.

Understanding what other people have to say can be helpful but only if applied to the individuals' unique proclivities and selves. Sacrifice of self must not take place, and any kind of idolization is destructive. Cultism of any kind is the antithesis of self-realization as it represents sacrifice of self and capitulation to morbid dependency.

Isn't it true that if we use time effectively we can dilute stress?

Giving yourself ample time to do things, to get from

one place to another, to complete jobs or tasks, to satisfy bodily necessities is vital to avoiding stress. However, it is even more important to be compassionate with yourself when "enough time" turns out to be "not enough" and when you find yourself inadvertently late in terms of any prearranged timetable whatsoever.

How is it possible to enhance or at least to invite or encourage another person's openness?

By being open yourself. Openness usually invites openness. However, there are people who are so threatened by the possibility of increased openness that they react with increased closure when in contact with an open person. Very detached people need a very longstanding relationship before openness on the part of a friend can have an ameliorative effect.

Doesn't openness and the free flow of energy result in a depletion of energy?

No. Fatigue and energy depletion are characteristic of being closed. Holding back takes a great deal of energy. Being open enhances relaxation and constantly replenishes energy.

However, energy used in attempted interaction with people who are not ready for interaction is wasted, and this kind of proselytizing activity leads to great frustration and fatigue.

In all human endeavors the choice of appropriate partners is very important. Willing, well-motivated students are a joy to teachers. People who are open to getting well make easy and enjoyable patients for doctors. Loving people are a joy to each other.

Is society becoming more competitive?

I believe that society is unfortunately becoming more competitive, more glory-seeking, and more pride-oriented. This is happening despite the fact that cooperative relating becomes mandatory for survival as populations increase and natural resources must be cherished and shared on an equitable basis. I believe that an increase in paranoia born of competition and pride in a world of ever-increasing technological advance is the greatest menace to our survival on the planet. Unfortunately, competition goes on as a self-stimulating and self-feeding malignancy.

There are people who are extremely uptight and constricted about spending small amounts of money but are utterly free in spending or investing huge amounts. What is the possible explanation of this behavior?

Large amounts of money for large things and large investments are felt by some people as being quite remote from themselves. Such expenditures are therefore not felt as self-depletion by people who "see money as blood." They also often see large expenditures as a conversion of money from one medium into another without loss of capital worth or personal wealth.

Small expenditures are seen as real expenditures, as money really going out rather than being converted into other forms. These expenditures are felt as personal ones, close to home, and as such are felt as real spending and a giving away of blood or self. Peculiarly, small expenditures and small amounts of money are felt as forms of intimate depletion—of giving away something very close to one's heart—while large amounts are "way out there" on the periphery of significant consciousness.

Differentiate between love, infatuation, possessiveness, and dependency.

Where they exist they overlap and delineating boundaries can be very difficult.

Dependency and possessiveness, and sometimes infatuation, too, are the antithesis of real love—love involving respect for and caring about the loved person and his or her real proclivities and needs. I think of these as anti-love, though our culture often promotes them and idealizes them as love and even as deep love. I also see them as largely serving neurotic needs—illusions, narcissistic preoccupations, and self-idealization—rather than promoting integration, homeostasis, and inner peace. Their hallmark is stress, strain, worry, vulnerability, fragility, and neurotic suffering, all the antithesis of a mellow, truly life-offering existence.

Real love, involving respect for separate selves and separate rhythms, tastes, needs, and proclivities, is based on mutual respect, knowledge of each other, kindness, and caring. This serves the purpose of self-realization and nourishes the possibility of inner peace.

Infatuation is often blind to the real identity of the partner, who is idealized in accordance with one's own needs rather than seen as a real person. This of course leads to disappointment and recrimination.

Possessiveness sees the partner, falsely, as a self-enhancing object. This form of narcissism disregards the separate self and humanity of the partner and makes for jealous tirades each time the partner does not act like one's own right hand.

Dependency makes for a form of attempted enslavement of the partner and promotes all kinds of impossible claims. "If you love me you will always understand me." "If you love me you will always choose to be with me, rather than anywhere else or with anyone else." As dependency increases, these claims become more bizarre and rages become increasingly powerful as claims are thwarted.

To add to the confusion, our culture subscribes to the notion that the greater one's jealousy and one's anger and one's pain, the greater one's love. Nothing could be farther from the truth. Pain, jealousy, and anger in this area are directly proportional to neurotic selfishness.

These ingredients of anti-love run rampant in all of us and create havoc wherever they exist. The ratio between real love and anti-love is a measure of health compared with sickness, a measure of constructive forces versus destructive forces in relating, and a measure of inner peace compared with inner chaos or mellow versus stressful living.

What if an emotional investment in a relationship turns out to have been too great relative to the way the relationship has evolved?

In some rare instances investment can be reduced through reasoning with oneself and through less frequent contact. Often this is not possible and termination of the relationship is necessary for one's well-being and even self-preservation. Sometimes complete and abrupt withdrawal is too painful and gradual disengagement is indicated. Of course wariness in making appropriate investments is indicated, as is extreme caution in avoiding exorbitant expectations.

What are the main characteristics of "mellow relating"?

Mellow relating is characterized by comfortable interchange of feelings and thoughts; mutual respect for each other's individuality, including needs, desires, proclivities, interests, moods, feelings, limitations, and assets; mutual interest in each other's constructive change and growth; care and help in reducing pain and in enhancing comfort and pleasure when feasible without undue self-sacrifice.

Is there a difference between "important work" and "serious work"?

The phrase "important work" usually alludes to efforts made in behalf of self-importance and the desire to amass power, money, prestige, fame, and admiration. In the context of this philosophy, important work is not important unless it happens to also be serious work.

"Serious work" is important because it is important to self. "Serious work" is soul satisfying. This means that it enhances change and growth and functions in behalf of self-realization. Any activity, or even a non-activity—for example, the relaxing use of leisure time —may be considered more serious than work if it works in behalf of ones real self.

Can kindness exist at one's own expense?

Not usually. Kindness contributes to fruitful relating and thus contributes to self-satisfaction. There are times when some self-sacrifice functions in behalf of the welfare of others, but this is not kindness if it is contrived for self-glorifying martyrdom.

Real kindness is not forced or willed. It is an extension of compassion for self and respect for the human condition. It comes comfortably and smoothly and is extended with nonpatronizing grace as part of good feelings generally. When there is inhibition or force involved in attempting to be kind, we must look for underlying cynicism, hopelessness, and paranoia; these require remedy before genuine kindness can become an easygoing, self-gratifying habit. If an objective act of kindness makes us feel foolish, vulnerable, helpless, depleted, weak, or "like a sucker," we have much serious work to do in the area of reconciliation with the human condition.

Is there any way to dilute a relationship besides infrequent contact?

To see the other individual only in the presence of other people can help. However, the most effective *dilution*, regardless of the exclusivity or frequency of contact, takes place when emotional investments and interest are withdrawn. Sometimes this can be done only through reinvestment in another person or persons.

If a deadlock occurs when a decision must be made regarding a particular action, can this philosophy provide an ingredient that would tilt the balance in one direction rather than the other?

If one direction contributes to decreasing stress on self, all other things being equal, this is the direction to take. Any decision or action that leads to a decrease in stress makes a valuable contribution to mellow living. The answer as to which direction feels less stressful usually comes quickly and easily if we don't permit intellectualizing, logical argument, and ruminating to get in our way. The idea is to go directly to our feelings. The main reasons we don't do this more often are: 1) we have largely abandoned the importance of feelings and immediate response in favor of logical calculation, and 2) complying with the society's success syndrome, we have placed personal well-being low in our order of priorities.

Is personal philosophy more valuable than "constructive direction" in working out our stressful conflicts?

Following even the most "constructive directions" is not only limited but can even be destructive if not accompanied by self-scrutiny and by a strong personal philosophy. Trading one set of "shoulds" for another, however valid the new shoulds are, does not provide autonomy and even threatens spontaneity.

A personal philosophy based on one's own observations, insights, and decisions is invaluable in bringing one's central self to life. It is invaluable in bringing back "deadened feelings," in breaking through automatic repression, in initiating and sustaining integration, and in providing a lasting bulwark against the inhuman values inherent in a disturbed society.

A personal philosophy can be a real philosophy and a constant source of nourishing strength in pursuing inner peace only if it is born of one's own struggle. This means that a philosophy's usefulness is directly proportional to the struggle one has made to develop that philosophy. Reading and listening to others is fine but ultimately one must struggle through to personal insights, beliefs, and motives in order to have a kinetic or working philosophy, or what I like to call a psychophilosophy. This is a philosophy that can change us psychologically and can change our lives in all respects. This kind of philosophy, based on one's own insights and beliefs, is crucial to finding relief from inner conflict, which cannot be resolved by means of superimposed shoulds, rules, or dictums, however wise or benevolently intended they may be.

How does the process of "getting even" start and what keeps it going?

We human beings are ingenious in our ability to initiate and to sustain intricate neurotic devices. This applies to the whole pride-idealized-image mechanism. Schematically put, it goes this way. Feeling hurt and inadequate, we develop a compensatory exalted image of ourselves, investing pride in many qualities that sustain the exaltation and the glory of the image: for example, pride in being the smartest, the most lovable, the strongest, the nicest, the most masculine or feminine, and so forth. If we fall from any of these positions we employ self-hate and self-lashing (see *Compassion and Self Hate*) to whip us back in line toward self-glorification again. We learn to use self-hate in this way, both from parents and from society, when hatred (reward and punishment) is used rather than understanding and insight in dealing with "shortcomings" and "transgressions." If any of our prides are hurt from the outside, we restore pride through hating the person who hurts us and putting him or her down and ourselves "up." We learn this, too, from parents and society through contact with confreres and adults.

The entire process constitutes "getting even" with

people and with aspects of the world that hurt our pride. All kinds of fantasies of "getting even" can often be traced to early childhood. Pride is restored in two ways: 1) through vindictive triumph over the enemy—kicking him down and elevating self, and 2) by withdrawal—not caring, leaving, pulling out and adopting an indifferent and superior attitude—and using this superiority to reestablish the pride position and the image. Of course these mechanisms in restoring pride also restore us to a position of vulnerability and cause us to be "set up to be knocked down" all over again, making inner peace and harmony tenuous if not impossible. A life devoted to guarding and compensating for hurt pride is one in which trust, either in self or in others, cannot exist. The tension and stress of being paranoid and on guard preclude real comfort, let alone giving nourishment to real self.

Can practicing *being open be helpful in* becoming *more open?*

Yes, but the full benefit of practice can come only as part of having insight into this dynamic. What is particularly helpful in "practicing" being open is the "risk" one takes with one's self and with others. When being open successfully brings no self-depletion or hurt, this gives much encouragement to practice openness with greater freedom and with increased ability to "let go" without trepidation.

Inasmuch as adaptation to new surroundings and situations entails stress, is there any argument for avoiding these new situations?

No! There is more stress in trying to cling to an untenable status quo. There is also stress and much energy expended in keeping one's self resigned and stultified. Of course frenetic, disorganized, and destructive changes may be born of anxiety and stress and may create still more anxiety and stress.

Much of the stress accompanying constructive moves comes from lack of insight into and acceptance of the time necessary to make adaptations—from expecting and demanding instant adaptations. If we give ourselves ample and appropriate time to adapt to new situations and do not respond to stress by becoming stressed at feeling stress we will experience changes in a much more relaxed, stress-reduced way.

Is there any particular enemy of inner peace that may be overlooked even by psychotherapy?

Inner peace cannot exist where there is an idealized and consequently distorted view of the human condition. People who essentially fail to know what it is to be a person must suffer from irreconcilable conflicts, vast disappointments, and intense self-hate whenever they encounter troublesome human characteristics: feelings; thoughts—appropriate and inappropriate; confusions; conflicts; fear; pleasure; sadness; helplessness; and every kind of impurity and temptation. No amount or kind of treatment can be helpful because each revelation of humanity will lead to revulsion and self-contempt if the frame of reference is not a realistic human one. Therefore, inner peace can come only if that frame of reference is changed. If a man who has a nose, an ordinary nose, does not know that other people have noses and believes that his nose is an abhorrent aberration, he will generate self-hate each time he sees his nose. Learning that noses and human beings are almost inseparable may be helpful. In short, people who don't know, who view human substance as dirty and nonhumanness as clean, must undergo profound educational revision. They must learn that whatever is human is appropriate, and whatever is God-like, saint-like, and "pure" is the stuff of emptiness, vacuum, and unreality, and is the enemy of inner peace.

Why do so many of us seem to have real comtempt for leisure time?

Too many people feel that they are doing something of secondary or little importance and are taking time off from the main goal (self-idealization and glorification) when they are not involved in direct accomplishment. Leisure time is of prime importance and must be regarded as such if it is to be used effectively. But for this to happen we must reduce the importance of accomplishment and running in competitive rat races.

Can we get rid of the pain of rejection?

Accepting the fact that all human beings are rejected at times, that being rejected is inevitable and no disgrace, is helpful. But giving up dependency, especially the quest to be taken care of by others, is curative.

Are there reconciliations other than those we make within ourselves that are of primary importance?

Internal reconciliations have primacy over all others. But this is not to minimize the importance of reconciling ourselves to all realities of the human condition and the world we live in. This is true of work, pleasure, and especially relationships. Reconciliation on a relating basis involves seeing, understanding, and accepting people with whom constructive relationships are possible, in all of their complexity, ramifications, and limitations.

This generally means that expectations must not be exorbitant. Reconciliation to life in any of its multifaceted aspects invariably involves appropriate insights about reality.

Fantasy living and illusion make reconciliation with the human condition impossible. This usually leads to disappointment and cynicism and sometimes to hopelessness and despair.

Isn't it possibly less stressful to comply with cultural dictums, to conform to the success-seeking we learned in childhood? Isn't this an easier road?

No. Obsessive habits antithetical to human characteristics and proclivities, especially those dedicated to never-ending attainment, are always severely stressful.

Habituation does not negate stress. Maladaptive practices, however familiar and habitual they become, continue to be destructive. The disturbed man who washes and scrubs his hands five hundred times a day complies with an inner dictate and is totally familiar with his compulsive habit. But this neither mitigates the anxiety that compels this practice nor prevents destruction to his hands, which become ulcerated and infected. Sisyphus, who in the ancient myth pushes a boulder up a hill all of his life, does not enjoy the practice simply because it has become familiar.

Initial efforts to change may produce stress but this soon gives way to a sense of well-being. This happens because knowing, just knowing, that we are doing, just doing, something really good for ourselves is a superb morale builder, gives us hope, and reduces stress. Changes that produce greater self-realization and compatibility with the human condition can't fail to augment inner peace and to reduce stress.

What other ingredients are characteristic of mutual loving or mutual caring?

In caring, we desire to struggle for mutual understanding and mutual satisfaction. We know that people, however much they love each other and care about each other, do not have identical natural rhythms, nor do they speak the same language. This means that differences in tastes, appetites, interests, proclivities, and desires abound. This further means that communication is not an easy, natural, God-given thing. People who are mature and who care are motivated to work and to struggle to build a common language in order to understand each other. They are motivated to help in each other's mutual satisfaction.

If people believe in and live by a given priority list, a compassionate one, in which self-caring comes before all else and people-caring comes before principles, don't they violate self-interest when they maintain the importance of people over personal principle?

Violation is an important term in this context. If we kill or even just hurt someone else in order to maintain principle, we seldom do so to sustain self. Self and self-enhancing principles seldom if ever require sacrifice of others on any level. Principles requiring sacrifice of others are almost always in violation of self and in the service of idealization, pride, and glory.

Can infatuation disturb inner peace?

In *real love* the other person is known and respected as the real person he or she is. *Infatuation* is at least in part a narcissistic activity. It represents a fixation with one's own projected ideal, and has little or nothing to do with the real person or object of one's "love." Indeed, it obscures the vision and resists real knowledge of the other person, let alone respect for who he or she really is. Contact with the other person as a reality often destroys the illusion and the so-called love. If the other person proves to be different, indeed very different, from the projected, distorted ideals, contempt and hatred may follow, as well as disappointment and despair. Infatuation and idealized love are usually the enemies of inner peace.

Why are so many people alienated, detached, and resigned?

These are prime cultural defenses designed to mitigate anxiety. They have evolved over many years through unconscious trial and error and in part they do work. We long ago found out that if you don't care you don't get hurt. Of course the price paid is staggering—relative deadness or pseudo-aliveness; stagnation; boredom and self-hate; and severely disturbed, attenuated relationships.

We perpetuate these neurotic defenses through our children from generation to generation. Thus we are victims of victims of victims. We teach our children to subvert themselves in favor of society's conventions and dictates so as not to "make waves." We unconsciously pass along the message that they should deaden themselves in order to become "successes," creating minimal disturbance to themselves and to us and whenever possible also feeding our pride. We teach them that we approve the painless quest for nondisturbing activity related to cultural concepts of success. Some of our children, in an effort to live on a more fully alive scale, become chronically and compulsively rebellious, but this too is a form of resignation, since it is a compulsive reaction to conformity. Compulsion is never a function of self-realization.

Is being loved—that is, having the feeling of being cared about—therapeutic?

Yes, but not nearly as much as loving and caring, which activate inner resources. People commonly ask, "Do you love me?" A more important question is, "Do you receive and feel my loving you?"

Why do so many people seem oblivious to the fact that they have reached the goals they started out with, and instead go on and on endlessly extending these goals in utterly ruthless ways in terms of consequences to themselves and others?

For example, there is the extraordinarily rich man who goes on to make still more money and fights to keep employees or colleagues from also enjoying the benefits of profits.

In a society that is essentially goal-oriented rather

than process-oriented, that is more concerned with the end product than with the means and conditions of attaining it, goals become the essential thing in life. Goals are equated with life. Competition and goals are equated with self, and people are felt as threats to self. Reaching a goal is felt with satisfaction at first but then is viewed with horror. This is so because the goal reached is the goal removed and this is felt as a loss of stimulus, as a loss of motivation, and as a loss of life itself. Therefore goals beyond goals are constructed and unnecessary competition takes place so as to provide still more of the addictive stuff of stimulation. It is not easy to give up the habit of a lifetime. It is not easy to broaden one's life. It is not easy to surrender pseudo-aliveness for the real thing (''real'' here pertains to self-realization, the aliveness of inner peace, and the aliveness and satisfactions born of cooperative relating). It is not easy but it can be done. I've seen it done, even by people who for years had been terrified both of other people and of themselves.

How can a decrease in competition make one's life more interesting and exciting?

A decrease in competition leads to inner peace and a personal state in which one's resources can be more fully appreciated and used. In competition we seldom use aspects of ourselves that are not directly applicable to areas of competition. These neglected areas of ourselves *come to life* as we attain removal from the rat race. Lessening the bonds of competition also restores our ability to be in touch with ourselves and tune in once again to our feelings, perceptions, desires, and pleasures.

As we become less competitive, so does our world, and the people of that world are seen less as adversaries and antagonists and more as confreres. This means that we can enjoy beauty, talent, and ability without feeling demeaned. I remember one highly competitive woman who felt demeaned by beautiful women, people who dressed well, people who articulated well, and even by museum paintings "done by others." As she became less competitive her world became a more beautiful one and more peacefully exciting than it had been for years.

Why do so many people seem to have considerable inhibition about doing "mindless things" and just plain relaxing?

This inhibition is fed by the same dynamic that demeans leisure time. Many people have pride invested in doing only things that are accomplishment-oriented. This "should" is almost always unconscious, but the self-hate that follows what is regarded as time used for trivia is usually felt on a conscious level.

Why do so many of us so willingly ignore, or even help in, the destruction of our own yearnings and tastes, and to what extent does this process destroy inner peace?

We give up our own tastes, proclivities, yearnings, and interests largely as a result of poor self-esteem and the compulsive need to be liked by others. This leads to compliance and conformity, which are antithetical to actual self, but which give a false sense of inner security and safety. The violation to self destroys inner peace. We cannot chronically violate the sensibilities and needs of real self without producing inner fragmentation and chaos. This is the antithesis of inner peace and a major contribution to chronic anxiety.

How can a person become more eclectic, that is, increasingly like different kinds of people, subjects, activities, and things?

This largely happens as an extension of greater self-acceptance. As we accept, cherish, and are more in touch with various aspects of ourselves, our interest in diverse people becomes possible also. This happens as a natural evolution and consequence of freeing ourselves from the threat of our own diversities.

Why are people often so secretive about many things that are commonplace and relatively superficial?

I think it's mostly to guard against potential hurt to sick pride. For example, I recently saw someone who is afraid to let anyone know that she is applying to medical school. She is afraid that, if she is rejected, her pride will be even more hurt if "they" find out. She will tell them only after she is certain of acceptance. This woman has much pride invested in success, as well as in never being rejected.

Are there limits to self-growth? To put it another way —can one get bigger than oneself?

There are limits to all things, probably even the universe. But as with the universe, we don't really know how "big" a self is. Therefore our involvement is with the process of growing itself—not pride-aggrandizement growing but self-realization growing. The deterrent to growth is pride. To the extent that we can rid ourselves of pride investments we make it possible to grow, especially in being more human to ourselves and to others.

To what extent can people be mutually helpful? In other words, are there limits to friendship?

There are limits to all aspects of the human condition. However close we become we are separate individuals and have separate needs. The amount of closeness and help that is possible depends on the people involved. An appropriate emotional investment in friendship can be fruitful; overinvestment usually leads to grievous disappointment and undue stress. In this connection it is important to be prudent, but not to the point of paranoia.

Can the reconciliation to death through feeling one's self as part of eternity also be a stratagem or rationalization?

Could be, and perhaps this is my own and other people's stratagem. But I think the struggle and feelings involved are all-important, what I would call the gut reaction. I think we know the difference. When actual confrontation and reconciliation have taken place, peace of mind follows. There is also change in feelings about one's self, the world, time, and the universe.

Does a common interest act to cement a good relationship?

Not always! Sometimes a common interest can be used as a vehicle for competition and also for mutual vilification. Much depends on just what the common interest is. Mutual kindness is a common interest of enormous value as is interest in the well-being of other people. I've known couples whose common interest was money and who vilified each other when there was a lack of it.

Does doing something we don't feel like doing lead to anxiety?

Obviously we can't always do what we want and must sometimes do what we don't feel like doing. Sometimes the practice of kindness even when we don't feel like it overcomes inertia in this area and generates feelings of kindness in us for ourselves as well as others.

If we "unthink" and do what we feel like doing won't we engage in many impulsive actions?

Don't think doesn't mean don't wait. We must wait for our feelings to clarify and to change also, if they do in fact change.

We must be cautious about any extreme behavior. For example, if we are tired, a vacation may be in order rather than a change in life-style.

What is good therapy for a person who hates himeslf?

Loving him more than he loves himself is good medicine.

Which takes precedence in human relating on a constructive level, fidelity or kindness?

Kindness takes precedence, but the two are not mutually exclusive; infidelity can be used unkindly and may even be a sadistic ploy.

Why do people get angry at people who are not "accomplishing" or "becoming" but who are happy just "being"?

Envy, especially in people who are compulsively driven, sometimes drives them to rage when they encounter people who can relax and be happy with themselves. Other people feel frustrated when in the presence of resigned people who are not accomplishing but who are not relaxed either—only pseudo-relaxed.

"Nonaccomplishment" does not preclude change and growth; both are quite consistent with a self-accepting, relaxed state, which must not be confused with compulsive resignation.

If self-love (real and not narcissistic—that is, to the exclusion of everyone else) is mending, is self-beating fragmenting?

Yes, in love, the self is involved as an integrated whole, comfortable with itself. In self-beating, one part of the self is split off in order to inflict punishment on the other, thus forming a division or fragmenting action.

What happens if competition is unavoidable?

Confrontations are often unavoidable in our society. Priorities are of prime importance. I refuse to injure myself or another person over a parking space. However, in unavoidable issues involving, for example, the defense of a loved one, in which hurt to someone else is inevitable, I think attitude is of extreme importance. To defend one's self with regret about having to hurt someone else is much less injurious to self than to do it with vindictive relish.

When does the desire for vindictive triumph begin in our society?

I think that, like "getting even" fantasies, often it begins in early childhood fantasies caused by hurt feelings the child has. In our culture many of these become firmly rooted because of economic impoverishment. The importance of money is stressed and this has an effect on children much earlier in life than most people suppose. But initial hurt feelings are connected with emotional deprivation and parental transgressions —real, exaggerated, and invented.

Is there any way other than sheer struggle added to insight to overcome strong inertia?

Sometimes a strong symbolic gesture to ourselves can be helpful. A patient I have who is an artist works on improving her studio and making it more comfortable when she suffers from inertia. This makes her feel good and serious about herself and her work and is shortly followed by her painting again.

Can habits be "good"?

Compulsive complying to "shoulds" is not good. The term "habit" has this connotation, and if a habit is in any way used to dilute spontaneity, this is not "good." But there are things we do in the service of real self almost automatically and habitually which are "good." Examples are: the habit of surrendering to proper care when we are sick, which can be lifesaving; the habit of relishing feeling good and personal peace; the habit of enjoying one's own company; the habit of taking a loss with relative equanimity and moving on; the habit of waiting for feelings to jell rather than acting on impulse; and the habit of periodically exploring habits so as to differentiate them from resigned should-oriented, self-stultifying compulsions.

How can we eliminate the need for "narcissistic supplies"?

It helps to struggle to help other people. But the principal aid is the development and evolution of one's own inner resources. As we tap our own abilities and give voice to our own proclivities and talents in the service of ourselves and others we have less need for stratagems to build false images of ourselves.

Is changing a life-style or way of life difficult?

Much depends on understanding, motivation, and degree of resistance. With increased and ever-growing insight into the constructive emotional and physical economy involved in change, resistance is lowered and change is easier. Of course some people need to change more than others. Some of us have been greater victims of society, family, and ourselves than others.

Unfortunately, people who need to change the most, often in order to survive, are usually most lacking in insight and are most resistant. But, nobody is hopeless! It must be kept in mind that real change takes practice and time and considerable struggle.

Change is not a straight road. We backtrack and sidetrack. A man who ran all of his life and now walks may find himself running now and then. But he will know the difference and understand the benefits of leisurely walking and will return to it more often and perhaps with greater ease.

In changing, it is good to remember that there is no goal to reach. The process of changing a life-style is more important than reaching a goal or measuring a performance. In other words, we don't arrive at a given spot and then stop. Instead, we continue to become increasingly mellow all the days of our lives. As we become reconciled to ourselves and to our world and universe, becoming more mellow gets easier and easier because we tend to fight against ourselves less and less.